Time Will Clean the Carcass Bones

ALSO BY LUCIA PERILLO

Lucia Perillo

Time Will Clean the Carcass Bones

Selected and New Poems

COPPER CANYON PRESS
Port Townsend, Washington

ACKNOWLEDGMENTS

"Yellow Claw" was reprinted in *Pushcart Prize XL: The Best of the Small Presses.*

Some of these poems previously appeared in *The American Poetry Review, Jung Journal, The New England Review, The New Yorker, Orion,* and *World Literature Today.*

"*Speckled and Silver" appeared in *The Book.*

Cover art: Digital photo by Jean Clottes, panel from Chauvet-Pont d'Arc Cave

Copper Canyon Press is in residence at Fort Worden State Park in Port Townsend, Washington, under the auspices of Centrum. Centrum is a gathering place for artists and creative thinkers from around the world, students of all ages and backgrounds, and audiences seeking extraordinary cultural enrichment.

LIBRARY OF CONGRESS CATALOGING-IN-PUBLICATION DATA

Perillo, Lucia Maria, 1958–
[Poems. Selections]
Time will clean the carcass bones : selected and new poems / Lucia Perillo.
    pages; cm
ISBN 978-1-55659-473-1 (hardcover)
ISBN 978-1-55659-502-8 (softcover)
1. Title.
PS3566.E69146A6   2016
811.54—dc23

2015034497

9 8 7 6 5 4 3 2 FIRST EDITION

COPPER CANYON PRESS
Post Office Box 271
Port Townsend, Washington 98368

www.coppercanyonpress.org

Contents

from *Inseminating the Elephant* (2009)

from *On the Spectrum of Possible Deaths* (2012)

New Poems

Everything in nature is lyrical in its ideal essence, tragic in its fate, and comic in its existence.

GEORGE SANTAYANA

Time Will Clean the Carcass Bones

from

Dangerous Life

(1989)

Ah, my friend, I sometimes think that I
lead a highly dangerous life, since I'm
one of those machines that can burst apart!

NIETZSCHE

The News (A Manifesto)

So today, yet another Guyanese will try to run the border
dressed in a dead housewife's hair—all they've recovered
since her disappearance in a downtown shopping mall.
An "incident," the paper says. Another "routine occurrence"—
wresting my trust from the publicans
assigned to keeping us safe, whole. Rather:
vow to stay vigilant against the maiming
that waits in each landscape, even in this
mundane procession of muddy spring days. To see
the tenacity of rooted hair for what it is:
an illusion as fleeting as courage. To keep the meat
between one's ribs from being torn, to keep the hard
marble of the cranium covered with its own skin.
To stay vigilant. To watch the signs of violence stirring
even in one's own machine. To keep both breasts
attached and undiseased. To keep the womb empty;
and yet to keep the organs living there
from shriveling like uneaten fruit, from turning
black and dropping. And not to mistake the danger
for a simple matter of whether
to put the body on the streets, of walking
or of staying home—; there are household cleansers
that can scar a woman deeper than a blade
or dumdum bullets. The kitchen drawers are full of tools
that lie unchaperoned. Even with the doors and windows
bolted, in the safety of my bed, I am haunted by the sound
of him (her, it, them) stalking the hallway,
his long tongue already primed with Pavlovian drool.
Or him waiting in the urine-soaked garages of this city's
leading department stores, waiting to deliver up the kiss

of a gunshot, the blunted kiss of a simple length of pipe.
But of course I mean a larger fear: the kiss
of amputation, the therapeutic kiss of cobalt.
The kiss of a deformed child. Of briefcase efficiency
and the forty-hour workweek. Of the tract home:
the kiss of automatic garage-door openers that
despite the dropped eyelid of their descent do nothing
to bar a terror needing no window for entry:
it resides within. And where do we turn for protection
from our selves? My mother, for example, recommends marriage—
to a physician or some other wealthy healer. Of course
it's him, leering from his station behind her shoulder,
who's making her say such things: the witch doctor,
headhunter, the corporate shaman, his scalpel
drawn & ready, my scalp his ticket out.

First Job/Seventeen

Gambelli's waitresses sometimes got down on their knees
searching for coins dropped into the carpet—
hair coiled and stiff, lips coated in that hennaed shade of red,
the banner-color for lives spent in the wake of husbands
dying without pensions, their bodies used in ceaseless
marching toward the kitchen's mouth, firm legs
migrating slowly ankleward. From that doorway,
Frankie Gambelli would sic a booze-eye on them,
his arms flapping in an earthbound pantomime of that
other Frank: The Swooned-Over. "You old cunts,"
he'd mutter. "Why do I put up with you old cunts?"—
never managing to purge his voice's tenor note
of longing. At me—the summer girl—he'd only stare
from between his collapsing red lids, eyes that were empty.

Once I got stiffed on a check when a man jerked
out of his seat, craned around, then bolted
from those subterranean women, sweaty and crippled
in the knees. Though I chased him up the stairs to the street,
the light outside was blinding and I lost the bastard
to that whiteness, and I betrayed myself with tears.
But coming back downstairs my eyes dried on another vision:
I saw that the dusk trapped by the restaurant's plastic greenery
was really some residual light of that brilliance happening
above us on the street. Then for a moment the waitresses
hung frozen in midstride—cork trays outstretched—
like wide-armed, reeling dancers, the whole
some humming and benevolent machine that knew no past, no future—
only balanced glasses, and the good coin in the pocket.
Sinatra was singing "Jealous Lover." All of us were young.

Dangerous Life

I quit med school when I found out the stiff they gave me
had book 9 of *Paradise Lost* and the lyrics
to "Louie Louie" tattooed on her thighs.

That morning as the wind was mowing
little ladies on a street below, I touched a Bunsen burner
to the Girl Scout sash whose badges were the measure of my worth:

Careers…
Cookery, Seamstress…
and *Baby Maker…* all gone up in smoke.

But I kept the merit badge marked *Dangerous Life,*
for which, if you remember, the girls were taken to the woods
and taught the mechanics of fire,

around which they had us dance with pointed sticks
lashed into crucifixes that we'd wrapped with yarn and wore
on lanyards round our necks, calling them our "Eyes of God."

Now my mother calls the pay phone outside my walk-up, raving
about what people think of a woman — thirty, unsettled,
living on food stamps, coin-op Laundromats & public clinics.

Some nights I take my lanyards from their shoebox, practice baying
those old camp songs to the moon. And remember how they told us
that a smart girl could find her way out of anywhere, alive.

The Revelation

I hit Tonopah at sunset,
just when the billboards advertising the legal brothels
turn dun-colored as the sun lies
down behind the strip mine.

And the whores were in the Safeway,
buying frozen foods and Cokes
for the sitters before their evening shifts.
Yes they gave excuses to cut
ahead of me in line, probably wrote bad checks,
but still they were lovely at that hour,
their hair newly washed
and raveling. If you follow
any of the fallen far enough
— the idolaters, the thieves and liars —
you will find that beauty, a cataclysmic
beauty rising off the face of the burning landscape
just before the appearance of the beast, the beauty
that is the flower of our dying into another life.
Like a Möbius strip: you go round once
and you come out on the other side.
There is no alpha, no omega,
no beginning and no end.
Only the ceaseless swell
and fall of sunlight on these rusted hills.
Watch the way brilliance turns
on darkness. How can any of us be damned.

from

The Body Mutinies

(1996)

—The people are like wolves to me!
—You mustn't say that, Kaspar.
 Look at Florian — he lost his father in an accident, he is blind,
 but does he complain? No, he plays the piano the whole day
 and it doesn't matter that his music sounds a little strange.

WERNER HERZOG
THE ENIGMA OF KASPAR HAUSER

How Western Underwear Came to Japan

When Tokyo's Shirokiya Dry Goods caught fire
in the thirties, shopgirls tore the shelves' kimonos
and knotted them in ropes. Older women used
both hands, descending safely from the highest floors
though their underskirts flew up around their hips.

The crowded street saw everything beneath—
ankles, knees, the purple flanges of their sex.
Versus the younger girls' careful keeping
one hand pinned against their skirts, against
the nothing under them and their silk falling.

Skin

Back then it seemed that wherever a girl took off her clothes
       the police would find her—
in the backs of cars or beside the dark night ponds, opening
       like a green leaf across
some boy's knees, the skin so taut beneath the moon
       it was almost too terrible,
too beautiful to look at, a tinderbox, though she did not know.
       But the men who came
beating the night rushes with their flashlights and thighs—
       they knew. About Helen,
about how a body could cause the fall of Troy and the death
       of a perfectly good king.
So they read the boy his rights and shoved him spread-legged
       against the car
while the girl hopped barefoot on the asphalt, cloaked
       in a wool rescue blanket.
Or sometimes girls fled so their fathers wouldn't hit them,
       their legs flashing as they ran.
And the boys were handcuffed just until their wrists had welts
       and let off half a block from home.

God for how many years did I believe there were truly laws
       against such things,
laws of adulthood: no yelling out of cars in traffic tunnels,
       no walking without shoes,
no singing any foolish songs in public places. Or else
       they could lock you in jail
or condemn your self and soul by telling both your lower-
       and uppercase Catholic fathers.

And out of all these crimes, unveiling the body was of course
        the worst, as though something
about the skin's phosphorescence, its surface as velvet
        as a deer's new horn,
could drive not only men but civilization mad, could lead us
        to unspeakable cruelties.
There were elders who from experience understood these things
        much better than we.
And it's true: remembering I had that kind of skin does drive me
        half-crazy with loss.
Skin like the spathe of a broad white lily
        on the first morning it unfurls.

Inseminator Man

When I call him back now, he comes dressed in the silver of memory,
silver coveralls and silver boots
and a silver hard hat that makes no sense.
The cows could not bombard his head,
though the Lilies and the Buttercups, the Jezebels and Mathildas,
avenged their lot in other ways
like kicking over a pail or stomping on his foot.
Blue welt, the small bones come unknitted,
the big toenail a black cicada peeling off its branch.

♦ ♦ ♦

It wasn't hard to understand their grudge, their harbor
        of accumulated hurts —
imagine lugging those big tits everywhere, year after year.
Balloons full of wet concrete
hung between their legs like scrotums, duplicate and puffed.
I remember grappling with the nipples
like a teenage boy in a car's backseat
and how the teats would always fill again before I could complete
        their squeezing-out.
At night, two floors above them in the half-demolished barn,
my hands ached and made me dream of cows that drained
until the little stool rose off the ground and I found myself
        dog-paddling in milk.

♦ ♦ ♦

The summer after college I'd gone off to live with women
who'd forsworn straight jobs and underwear and men.

At night the ten of us linked hands
around a low wire-spool table before we took our meal of
            vegetables and bread.
Afterward, from where the barn's missing wall
opened out on Mad River, which had no banks but cut an oxbow
flush with the iridescent swale of the lower fields,
I saw women bathing, their flanks in the dim light
rising like mayflies born straight out of the river.

                    ◆ ◆ ◆

Everyone else was haying the lower field when he pulled up,
his van unmarked and streamlined like his wares:
vials of silvery jism from a bull named Festus
who — because he'd sired a Jersey that took first place
at the Vermont State Fair in '53 —
was consigned to hurried couplings with an old maple stump
rigged up with white fur and a beaker.
When the man appeared I was mucking stalls in such heat
that I can't imagine whether or not I would have worn
            my shirt
or at what point it became clear to me that the bull Festus
            had been dead for years.

                    ◆ ◆ ◆

I had this idea the world did not need men:
not that we would have to kill them personally,
but through our sustained negligence they would soon die off
like houseplants. When I pictured the afterlife
it was like an illustration in one of those Jehovah's Witness magazines,
all of us, cows and women, marching on a promised land
colored that luminous green and disencumbered by breasts.
I slept in the barn on a pallet of fir limbs,

ate things I dug out of the woods,
planned to make love only with women, then changed my mind
when I realized how much they scared me.

◆ ◆ ◆

"Inseminator man," he announced himself, extending a hand,
though I can't remember if we actually spoke.
We needed him to make the cows dry off and come into new milk:
we'd sell the boy-calves for veal, keep the females for milkers,
and Festus would live on, with this man for a handmaid,
whom I met as he was either going into the barn or coming out.
I know for a fact he didn't trumpet his presence,
        but came and went mysteriously
like the dove that bore the sperm of God to earth.

◆ ◆ ◆

He wore a hard hat, introduced himself before I took him in,
and I remember how he graciously ignored my breasts while still
        giving them wide berth.
Maybe I wore a shirt or maybe not: to say anything
        about those days now sounds so strange.
We would kill off the boys, save the females for milkers I figured
as I led him to the halfway mucked-out stalls, where he
        unfurled a glove past his elbow
like Ava Gardner in an old-movie nightclub scene.
Then greased the glove with something from a rusted can
        before I left him in the privacy of barn light
with the rows of cows and the work of their next generation
while I went back outside to the shimmering and nearly
        blinding work of mine.

Tripe

We were never a family given to tongue or brains.
So the cow's stomach had to bear her last straws,
had to be my mother's warning-bell that chops and roasts
and the parched breasts of chickens, the ribs and legs
and steaks and fish and even the calf's sour liver
had become testaments to the monotony of days.
Since then I have understood the rebellion hedged
in its bifurcated rind, its pallor, its refusal
to tear or shred when chawed on by first
the right then the left jaw's teeth —
until finally the wad must be swallowed whole.

The tough meat meant life's repertoire had shrunk
to a sack inside of which she was boxing shadows —
kids and laundry, yes, but every night the damned
insistence of dinner. And wasn't the stomach
a master alchemist: grass and slops and the green dirt
transformed into other cuts of bloody, marbled beef.
Times when she wanted that same transformation
the house filled with its stewing, a ghastly sweet
that drove us underneath the beds. From there
we braved mushroom clouds rising off her electric range,
blowing the kitchen walls as wide as both Dakotas.
And I pictured her pale-faced & lustrous with steam
as she stood in that new open space, lifting
the hair off her neck as the stockpot billowed
its sugary haze like the sweat of a hired man.

At St. Placid's

She wears a habit the unlikely blue color
of a swimming pool, the skin of her face
smooth where it shows beneath a wimple
from which one blond strand escapes.
While she squints at the sun, her hands
knit themselves in the folds of her skirts.
The man she's speaking to, the monk,
is also young, his shoulders broad
from shooting baskets in the gym.
I have seen him running across the fields
in his nylon shorts, big muscles like roasts
sheathing the bones in his thighs.
They are standing on the monastery's walkway
and I am at the window watching
this moment when their voices fall away,
nothing left but the sound of water dripping
off the trees, a fuchsia brooding in a basket
over her left shoulder. Silent now,
they are thinking. But not
about that. The fine weather, yes,
the church bells, the cross, an old woman
who used to come to Mass who's dying.
All this they think of. But surely
not about that, no. Not that other thing.

The Roots of Pessimism in Model Rocketry, the Fallacy of Its Premise

X-Ray had a see-thru payload chamber.
The Flyer Saucer model was a gyp —
unless you were the kind of kid who loved
the balsa wood shredding more than flight time,
the smashing down more than the going up.
When Big Bertha sheared my brother's pinkie
I watched medicine make its promise good:
in the future we would all be androids.
The doctors reinstalled his milky nail
and drained blue fingertip, though afterward
I felt a little cheated. Already
I'd envisioned how his mutant terrors
could be put to my use, the naked stub
unsheathed to jinx an enemy sneaker.

We were a tribe of Josef Mengeles
doing frontier science: putting crickets
in the payload, betting if they'd return
alive or dead. I always bet on death
because they always came down dead. I was
the pessimist, the child of many coins.
When someone fished from the dusty ballfield
the cocktail sausage of my brother's loss,
I gave its odds less than even money.
My vote was: Put the finger in a can,
send it to Estes Model Rocket Co.
who would feel guilty enough to send cash.
But guilt turned on me. Now my brother's hand
looks perfect, except when he makes a fist.

The Body Mutinies

outside St. Pete's

When the doctor runs out of words and still
I won't leave, he latches my shoulder and
steers me out doors. Where I see his blurred hand,
through the milk glass, flapping goodbye like a sail
(& me not griefstruck yet but still amazed: how
words and names — medicine's blunt instruments—
undid me. And the seconds, the half seconds
it took for him to say those words). For now,
I'll just stand in the courtyard, watching bodies
struggle in then out of one lean shadow
a tall fir lays across the wet flagstones.
Before the sun clears the valance of gray trees
and finds the surgical-supply shop's window
and makes the dusty bedpans glint like coins.

from *The Body Mutinies*

Kilned

I was trying to somehow keep [my early pieces] true to their nature, to allow the crudeness to be their beauty. Now I want the lava to teach me what it does best.

STEPHEN LANG

These days when my legs twitch like hounds under the sheets
and the eyes are troubled by a drifting fleck —
I think of him: the artist
who climbs into the lava runs at Kalapana,
the only person who has not fled from town
fearing the advance of basalt tongues.
He wears no special boots, no special clothes,
no special breather mask to save him
from poison fumes. And it is hot, so hot
the sweat drenches him and shreds his clothes
as he bends to plunge his shovel
where the earth's bile has found its way to surface.
When he catches fire, he'll roll in a patch of moss
then simply rise and carry on. He will scoop
this *pahoehoe,* he will think of Pompeii
and the bodies torqued in final grotesque poses.
Locals cannot haul away their wooden churches fast enough,
they call this the wrath of Madame Pele,
the curse of a life that was so good
they should have known to meet it with suspicion.
But this man steps into the dawn and its yellow flames,
spins each iridescent blue clod in the air
before spreading it on a smooth rock ledge to study.
First he tries to see what this catastrophe is saying.
Then, with a trowel in his broiling hand,
he works to sculpt it into something human.

Women Who Sleep on Stones

Women who sleep on stones are like
brick houses that squat alone in cornfields.
They look weatherworn, solid, dusty,
torn screens sloughing from the window frames.
But at dusk a second-story light is always burning.

Used to be I loved nothing more
than spreading my blanket on high granite ledges
that collect good water in their hollows.
Stars came close without the trees
staring and rustling like damp underthings.

But doesn't the body foil what it loves best?
Now my hips creak and their blades are tender.
I can't rest on my back for fear of exposing
my gut to night creatures who might come along
and rip it open with a beak or hoof.

And if I sleep on my belly, pinning it down,
my breasts start puling like baby pigs
trapped under their slab of torpid mother.
Dark passes as I shift from side to side
to side, the blood pooling just above the bone.

Women who sleep on stones don't sleep.
They see the stars moving, the sunrise, the gnats
rising like a hairnet lifted from a waitress's head.
The next day they're sore all over and glad
for the ache: that's how stubborn they are.

from *The Body Mutinies*

Compulsory Travel

Not yet did we have personalities to interfere
with what we were: two sisters, two brothers.
Maybe our parents really were people who walked in the world,
were mean or kind, but you'd have to prove it to us.
They were the keepers of money, the signers of report cards,
the drivers of cars. We had a station wagon.
Back home we even had a dog, who was fed
by a neighbor kid while we toured the Jersey shore.
We waded in the motel pool and clung
to the edge of the deep end, because we couldn't swim.
Maybe that's why we never went in the ocean, despite
hours of driving. We could've just gone down the block!
Yet each year we made a ritual of this week
spent yelling and cursing and swatting each other,
with none of the analyses we now employ, the past
used as ammunition, the glosses from our latest therapist.
Back then a sock in the jaw could set anyone straight.

On Sunday afternoon, the homeward traffic would grind still
where the turnpike bottlenecked. My father
would slam his forehead against the steering wheel,
start changing lanes and leaning on the horn.
Without breeze through the window, the car would hold
our body heat like an iron skillet, skin peeling
from our burned shoulders as we hurled pretzels
and gave the finger to kids stopped in cars beside us.
My mother wouldn't mention the turn we'd missed
a few miles back; instead she'd fold the map
and jam it resolutely in the glove box while we crept on.
Perhaps this was our finest hour, as the people

we were becoming took shape and began to emerge:
the honkers of horns and the givers of fingers.
After the sun turned red and disappeared, we rolled
through darkness, wondering if the world knew all its names:
Wickatunk, Colts Neck, Zarephath, Spotswood—in every town
there were houses, in every house there's a light.

Limits

The dead man.
Every now and again, I see him.
And the wildlife refuge where I worked then,
the shallow ponds of Leslie Salt Company
patchworking the San Francisco Bay edges
and spreading below the hills like broken tiles,
each pond a different color — from blue to green
to yellow until finally the burnished red
of terra-cotta, as the water grew denser
and denser with salt. Dunlins blew upward
like paper scraps torn from a single sheet,
clouds of birds purling in sunlight, harboring
the secret of escaped collision. And
that other mystery: how these weightless tufts
could make it halfway to Tierra del Fuego
and back before spring's first good day.
On those good days, a group from the charity ward
named after the state's last concession to saints
would trudge up the hill to the visitor center,
where I'd show them California shorebirds
— a stuffed egret, western sandpiper, and avocet —
whose feathers were matted and worn to shafts
from years of being stroked like puppies.
As I guided their hands over the pelts
questions stood on my tongue — mostly
about what led them to this peculiar life,
its days parceled into field trips
and visits to the library for picture books
with nurses whose enthusiasms were always greater
than their own. Their own had stalled out

before reaching the moist surface of their eyes,
some of the patients fitting pigeonholes built
in my head, like *Down syndrome* and *hydrocephalus*.
But others were not marked in any way,
and their defects cut closer to the bones
under my burnt-sienna ranger uniform.
Maybe I was foolish to believe in escape
from the future carried in their uncreased palms:
our lives overseen by the strict, big-breasted nurse
who is our health or our debts or even
our children, the *her* who is always putting crayons
and lumps of clay in our hands, insisting
we make our lives into some crude but useful thing.
And one day a man, a patient who must have been
supervised by his strict heart, fell down
suddenly and hard, on his way up the hill.
Two nurses prodded him on toward the building,
where he went down again like a duffel bag full of earth
in front of the reception desk where I was sitting.
I watched the one male nurse turn pale as ash
when he knelt to certify the heartbeat
of this man whose lips were blue and wet.
The other nurse took the group to the auditorium,
saying *James isn't feeling very well right now.*
James is sick. Get away from him. Then I heard
the dopey music of the automated slide show
behind those doors from which she never reappeared.
The male nurse was too young to leave stranded
with a man down on the smooth wood floor:
his cheek still velvet, his dark fingers
worrying the valleys of the man's white wrist.
He's okay, he's breathing, as the man's skin
turned gray, his mouth open, a cherry sore
at either edge. I don't remember what I did at first,

I must have puttered off to perform some
stupid task that would seem useful —
gathering premoistened towelettes
or picking up the phone while the nurse repeated
He's okay, he's breathing. But the colors
got worse until nothing could spare me
from having to walk my hand in the crease
of the man's blue throat, where his carotid
should have pulsed. Nothing.
I said *You breathe for him and I'll compress*,
and for a while we worked together like a clumsy
railroad handcar, me humping at arm's length
over the ribs, the nurse sealing his lips around
the man's scabbed mouth, while yellow mucus
drained from James's eyes and nose and throat.
Each time the nurse pressed his mouth to the man's
like a reluctant lover, the stink of cud
was on his lips when he lifted up. Sometimes
he had to hold his face out to the side,
to catch a few breaths of good salt air.
Until he was no longer able to choke back his gut
and asked whether I would trade places with him.
For a moment I studied the man's staved chest,
which even my small knuckles had banged to jelly,
then the yellow pulp that flecked the nurse's lips,
that sour, raw smell from their mix of spit.
And I said: *No. I don't think I could...*

It's strange what we do with the dead
— burning them or burying them in earth —
when the body always tries to revert to water.
Later, a doctor called to say the man's heart
had exploded like a paper sack: death hooked him
before he even hit the floor. So everything we did

was useless — we might as well have banged a drum
and blown into a horn. And notice how I just said "we" —
as though the nurse and I had somehow married
spirits in a pact of gambled blood, when in truth
the nurse, like the man, rode off in an ambulance,
the man for a pointless go-round in the ER, the nurse
for a shot of gamma globulin, while I stood
in the parking lot, picking lint off my shirt.
End of story. Except that since then James
has followed me, showing up sometimes at the house
to read my gas meter, sometimes behind the counter
where I ask him what I owe. No surprise then
that I've made my life with another James,
who swears my biggest defect is still the limits
on what I'll bring myself to do for someone else.
I know there are people who'll cut out their kidney
to replace a friend's cankered one, people
who'll rush into burning buildings to save the lives
of strangers. But every time I ponder selflessness
I hear the beats of my heart, that common loon,
most primitive of birds. Then my life seems most
like a naked, frail thing that must be protected,
and I have suddenly become its mother, paddling
with my own life saddled on my back.
There's one last thing I didn't mention —
when I refused to breathe for the dying James
what happened next was that I began to laugh:
a thin laugh, nervous laugh… but loud enough
to drift outside, where it stood on the hill
and creaked its wings a minute before lifting—
over the levees, across those shallowest of waters.

Needles

So first there's the chemo: three sticks, once a week,
      twenty-six weeks.
Then you add interferon: one stick, three times a week,
      forever.
And then there's the blood tests. How many blood tests?
      (Too many to count.)
Add all the sticks up and they come down to this: either
      your coming out clean
or else... well, nobody's talking
      about the B-side,
an *or else* that plows through your life like a combine
      driven at stock-car speed,
shucking the past into two piles: *things that mattered*
      and *things that didn't.*
And the first pile looks so small when you think of
      everything you haven't done —
never seeing the Serengeti or Graceland, never running
      with the bulls in Spain.
Not to mention all the women you haven't done yet!—
      and double that number of breasts.
Okay—
      you've got a woman, a good woman, make no mistake.
But how come you get just one woman when you're getting
      many lifetimes' worth of sticks?
Where is the justice in that? You feel like someone
      who's run out of clean clothes
with laundry day still half a week away; all those women
      you tossed in the pile
marked *things that didn't matter,* now you can't help but
      drag them out.

Like the blond on trail crew who lugged the chain saw
		on her shoulder up a mountain
and bucked up chunks of blighted trees — how could you
		have forgotten
how her arms quaked when the saw whined and the muscles
		went liquid in her quads,
or the sweaty patch on her chest where a mosaic formed
		of shiny flies and moss?
Or that swarthy-haired dancer, her underpants hooked
		across her face like the Lone Ranger,
the one your friends paid to come to the table, where
		she pawed and made you blush:
How come yer getting married when you could be muff-diving
		every night?
At college they swore it was John Dewey, they swore
		by the quadruped Rousseau,
and it took cancer to step up and punch your gut
		before you figured
that all along immortal truth's one best embodiment
		was just
some sixteen-year-old table-dancing on a forged ID
		at Ponders Corners.
You should have bought a red sports car, skimmed it under
		the descending arms at the railroad crossing,
the blond and brunette beside you under its moonroof
		and everything smelling of leather —
yes yes—this has been your flaw: how you have always
		turned away from the moment
your life was about to be stripped so the bone of it
		lies bare and glittering.
You even tried wearing a White Sox cap to bed but its bill
		nearly put your wife's eye out.
So now you're left no choice but going capless, scarred;
		you must stand erect;

you must unveil yourself as a bald man in that most
        treacherous darkness.
You remember the first night your parents left town, left
        you home without a sitter.
Two friends came over and one of them drove the Mercury
        your dad had parked stalwartly
in the drive (you didn't know how yet) — took it down
        to some skinny junkie's place
in Wicker Park, cousin of a friend of a cousin, friend
        of a cousin of a friend,
what did it matter but that his name was Sczabo.
        Sczabo! —
as though this guy were a skin disease, or a magician
        about to make doves appear.
What he did was tie off your friends with a surgical tube,
        piece of lurid chitterling
smudged with grease along its length. Then needle, spoon —
        he did the whole bit,
it was just like in the movies, only your turn turned you
        chicken (or were you defiant? —)
Somebody's got to drive home, and that's what you did
        though you'd never
made it even as far as the driveway's end before your dad
        put his foot over the transmission hump
to forestall some calamity he thought would compromise
        the hedges.
All the way back to Evanston you piloted the Mercury
        like General Montgomery in his tank,
your friends huddled in the backseat, spines coiled,
        arms cradled to their ribs —
as though each held a baby being rocked too furiously
        for any payoff less than panic.
It's the same motion your wife blames on some blown-out
        muscle in her chest

when at the end of making love she pitches violently,
        except instead of saying
something normal like *god* or *jesus* she screams *ow! ow!*
        and afterward,
when you try sorting out her pleasure from her pain,
        she refuses you the difference.
Maybe you wish you took the needle at Sczabo's place —
        what's one more stick
among the many you'll endure, your two friends not such
        a far cry from being women,
machines shaking and arching in the wide backseat
        as Sczabo's doves appeared —
or so you thought then, though now you understand
        all the gestures the body will employ
just to keep from puking. Snow was damping the concrete
        and icing the trees,
a silence stoppered in the back of your friends' throats
        as you let the Mercury's wheel pass
hand over hand, steering into the fishtails, remembering
        your dad's admonition:
when everything goes to hell the worst you can do
        is hit the brakes.

Monorail

Seattle, at the old World's Fair

He stands by the helm, his face full of blue
from the buildings at twilight, his hand
knuckled around a metal pole that keeps him
from falling, as he flies past the vaults
of startled mannequins, the red ohs of their lips.
Christmas lights are also falling
through the windshield, onto his chest:
right side green, left side red —
dark then back again.

Wait… my father is not moving yet:
no one has claimed the worn leather throne.
But his thoughts are moving, wondering
whether movement is the same as growing old
in the province of space, not time. Inside his shoes,
his toes are as blue as the city streets,
and the drum in his chest, his red-lit chest,
is growing dim. He knows the train he's about to ride
has one rail: no steering, no turns.
And the only skill is in the brake.

The brake. His lips roll over the words:
the dead man's brake. And a small boy
— come to ride up front — hears him,
tugs my father's coat and asks:
Hey mister, are you the driver of this train?

Cairn for Future Travel

I was young for a minute, but then I got old.
Already the black cane stands by
the threshold, already my feet are flowerpots
in thick black shoes. So not long now
before I will have what follows:

a spidery hairnet to circle my scalp, a hand
callused enough to whack your ear. And with them,
the deep wisdom of Sicilian great-aunts:
how to plumb for the melon's ripeness, how
to stand the loaves upright in my twine sack.

And you, are you ready? Have you brushed
your brown suitcoat and hat? Have you counted
your mahogany chessmen and oiled the zipper
on their leather case? Have you filled
your sack of crumbs for the pigeons?

In the park, men are waiting, raking
the bocce-court sand. And as for this second-floor
window where I shake my fist: soon you will learn
to feign deafness, fishing the silver ball
up from your loose, deep pocket.

from

The Oldest Map with the Name America

(1999)

The printing press could disseminate, but it could not retrieve.
To his annoyance, Waldseemüller himself learned the fantastic,
irreversible reach of this new technology. When Waldseemüller
changed his mind and decided that after all Amerigo Vespucci
should not be credited as the true discoverer of the New World,
it was too late.... The printed messages advertising America
were already diffused into a thousand places and could not
be recalled.

DANIEL J. BOORSTIN, *THE DISCOVERERS*

Beige Trash

Who is to blame for there being no tractors
churning the soil into veils
to drape over the telling
where and how I grew, in a suburb
with no men that I could in good conscience adorn
with prosthetic limbs or even crushed straw hats?
Kudzu was something we shouted
jujitsuing air like the Green Hornet's sidekick

whose name still needed some time to ferment
in those years separating the yellow peril
from kung-fu mania, before BRUCE LEE
floated up to the marquee lights.
Like the stripers you could not eat
floating on top of the poisonous river,
to whose bank we never carried our burdens
and let them weep down into Jersey.

Because surely these words would have profited
from at least one silo lording over,
with some earthmoving equipment
parked nearby in a nest of wire
belonging to some good old boy named...
what? Leldon? Lemuel? But sorry:
in no barn did the whiskey bottles lie
like Confederate casualties at Appomattox —

no tent revivals, no cousins with red hair
and freckled hands, no words as exotic as *po'boy*
or *chifforobe* or *muffuletta*. Which meant

we had no means to wrangle Beauty
into the cathedrals of our mouths,
though on occasion an ordinary cow
could make the car's eight-chambered heart
stop dead beside a pasture, where none of us

dared get out for fear of stampedes or hay fever
or maybe even fangs hidden behind the lips.
Call us ignorant: everything we knew poured out
those two-at-a-time black-and-white TVs —
one for picture, one for sound — & antlered
with coat hangers that gave even *Hawaii Five-O*
the speckling of constant winter. The snow
fell like the fur of our fat white dog

for whom my mother cooked lamb chops every night
in an attempt to cure its baldness,
while we dug our fingers in the chopmeat
before she slapped it into patties.
Then *Star Trek* came on. Then for an hour
the men faded in and out of light.
And there is nothing about this past
it does any service to the language to recall:

Art was what the fire department sold tickets to,
raising money for the hook and ladder.
It took place inside the school auditorium,
where an old Italian couple hid
by donning black and standing
just outside the purple spotlight.
Then music surged that was vaguely familiar
though we'd fail to lure its elaborate name

in from the borders of what we knew,
while the marionette-swan bobbled to its feet
as if newly born. I can say it now:
Tchaikovsky. Of course, the whole time
they worked the sticks and strings,
the puppeteers stood right out in the open.
Yet how silently they moved, how easy
a thing they were to pretend we couldn't see.

Foley

It is Harrison Ford who just saved the world,
but when he walks down a dirt road toward the ultralarge sun
what sound like his boots are really bricks being drudged
through a boxful of coffee beans. And the mare you've seen
clopping along those nineteenth-century cobbles —
she's a coconut struck by a ball-peen hammer.
And the three girls riding in the hansom,
where the jouncing rustles their silk-and-bone:
that's a toothbrush moving across birchbark.
Even the moment when one kickboxer's perfect body
makes contact with the other kickboxer's perfect body
has nothing to do with kickboxing, or bodies,
but the concrete colliding with the abstract of perfection,
which molts into a leather belt spanking a side of beef.
This is the problem with movies:
go to enough of them and pretty soon the world
starts sounding wrongly synced against itself: e.g.,
last night when I heard a noise below my bedroom window
that sounded like the yowl a cat would make
if its tongue were being yanked backward out its ass.
Pain, I thought. *Help,* I thought,
so at two a.m. I went outside with a flashlight
and found a she-cat corkscrewed to a tom,
both of them humped and quivering where the beam flattened
against the grass whose damp was already wicking
through my slippers. *Aaah… love,* I thought,
or some distantly cousined feline analogue of love,
or the feline analogue of the way love came out of the radio
in certain sixties pop songs that had the singer keening
antonyms: how can something so right feel so wrong,

so good hurt so bad… you know what I'm talking about.
And don't you think it's peculiar:
in the first half of the sixties they made the black girl-groups
sing with white accents and in the second half of the sixties
they made the white girl-groups sing with black accents,
which proves that what you hear is always
some strange alchemy of what somebody thinks you'll pay for
and what you expect. Love in particular
it seems to me we've never properly nailed down
so we'll know it when we hear it coming, the way
screaming "Fire!" *means* something to the world.
I remember this guy who made noises against my neck
that sounded like when after much tugging on a jar lid
you stick a can opener under its lip—that little *tsuck*.
At first I thought this must be
one of love's least common dialects, though later
when I found the blue spots all over I realized
it was malicious mischief, it was vandalism, it was damage.
Everybody has a story about the chorus of these,
love's faulty hermeneutics: the muffler in retreat
mistaken for the motor coming, the declaration
of loathing construed as the minor reproach;
how "Babe, can I borrow five hundred bucks?"
gets dubbed over "Goodbye, chump"—of course,
of course, and you slap your head but it sounds funny,
not enough sizzle, not enough snap. If only
Berlitz had cracked the translations or we had conventions
like the international code of semaphores;
if only some equivalent of the Captain Midnight decoder ring
had been muscled across the border. As it has
for my friend who does phone sex
because it's a job that lets her keep at her typewriter all day,
tapping out poems. Somehow she can work
both sides of her brain simultaneously, the poem

being what's really going on and the sex being what sounds
like what's going on; the only time she stops typing
is when she pinches her cheek away from her gums,
which is supposed to sound like oral sex
though she says it's less that it really *sounds* like oral sex
than that these men have established a pact, a convention
that permits them to *believe* it sounds like oral sex.
When they know
it's a woman pinching her cheek and not a blow job,
it's a telephone call and not a blow job,
it's a light beam whistling down a fiber, for god's sake,
and not a blow job. Most days I'm amazed
we're not all schizophrenics, hearing voices
that have been edited out of what calls to us
from across the fourth wall. I've heard
that in *To Have and Have Not* Lauren Bacall's singing
comes from the throat of a man; also that Bart Simpson is really
a middle-aged woman; and last week not once but twice
I heard different women wailing
in public parking lots, the full throttle
of unrestrained grief, and both times I looked straight at them
and pretended nothing unusual was going on,
as though what I was hearing were only the sound of air
shrieking through the spoiler on someone's Camaro.
That's also part of the pact my friend's talking about,
not to offer condolence, not to take note.
You don't tell the men they're sorry creatures,
you don't ask the women what went wrong.
If you're being mugged or raped or even killed
you have to scream "Fire!" instead of "Help!"
to get someone to help you. Though soon, if not already,
all the helpers will have caught on
and then you'll have to start screaming something else,
like that you've spotted Bacall or Harrison Ford on the street,

Bart Simpson even—no wait a minute, he's not real,
though I remember a time when even the president talked about him
as if he were human. It's not the sleaziness
of phone sex I bristle at, but rather the way it assists
the world in becoming imprecise
about what is real and what is not, what is a blow job
and what is only my friend jimmying her finger
in her mouth or making a sucky noise
against the back of her hand. Which is oddly exactly
how the professor of the ornithology class I took my junior year
taught us to lure birds in, because birds
would think these were the sounds of other birds.
And in that other life of mine,
when bird-watching was something I did for a living,
I remember packing high into the mountains
before the snow melted, when the trail couldn't be followed,
so mine would be the only soul for miles.
One reason I went up there was because at sundown
when the wind climbed the backs of the mountains
along with the spreading violet light,
you could hear the distinct murmuring that the Indians said
was the collective voices of the dead. And I'd lie there,
just my sleeping bag and pad set down on snow,
and I'd look hard at the sky, as though
the wind were something I could see if I looked hard enough,
listening equally hard to convince myself
about the voices of the dead, though always
I was tugged back from true belief
by the one side of my brain that insisted: *Wind.*
And also I remember
how once at the trailhead a man popped out of his motor home
and pointed a camcorder at me, asking
where I was going, what I was doing—though of course,
alone, I wasn't going to say.

But even as I turned away, I heard
the whir of the movie being made
and the man making up his own narration: *see this little girl,*
she says she's going to climb a mountain,
and briefly I thought about pulling a Trotsky on him
with my ice ax. But as the New Agers say I
"let it go," and I left,
and he didn't follow me, and nothing bad ever happened,
though from time to time I think about strangers watching that movie
in the man's living room, his voice overdubbing
(*see this little girl, she says she's going to climb a mountain*)
the sound of me, of my boots walking.

Air Guitar

The women in my family were full of still water;
they churned out piecework as quietly as glands.
Plopped in America with only the wrong words
hobbling their tongues, they liked one thing
about the sweatshop, the glove factory,
and it was this: you didn't have to say much.
All you had to do was stitch the leather fingers
until you came up with a hand; the rest
they kept tucked to their ribs like a secret book.
Why, was not said, though it doesn't seem natural
the way these women ripped the pages out
and chewed them silently and swallowed — where
is the ur-mother holding court beside her soup pot,
where are Scheherazade and the rest of those Persians
who wove their tragedies in rugs?
Once I tutored a Cambodian girl: each week
I rolled the language like a newspaper and used it
to club her on the head. In return she spoke
a mangled English that made all her stories sad,
about how she'd been chased through the jungle
by ruthless henchmen of Pol Pot; for months
she and her sisters mother grandmothers aunts
lived in the crowns of trees and ate what grew there
and did not touch down. When she told the story,
the way her beautiful and elaborately painted face
would loosen at each corner of her eyes and mouth
reminded me of a galosh too big for its shoe.
It was rubbery, her face, like the words
that sometimes haunt me with their absence,
when I wake up gargling the ghost of one

stuck like a wild hair far back in my mouth.
This morning it took me till noon to fish out
cathexis, and even then I did not know
what this meant until I looked it up.
As it was not until I met her sister
that I learned what the girl was telling me
was not the story she was telling: there were
no women in trees, no myrmidons of Comrade Pot,
their father was, is, had always been,
a greengrocer in Texas. Cathexis:
fixing emotional energy on some object
or idea — say the jungle, or the guy
getting rubbery with a guitar that isn't there.
Yet see how he can't keep from naming
the gut that spills above his belt *Lucille* —
as music starts to pour from his belly
and the one hiked-up corner of his lip. This
is part of the legend we tell ourselves about the tribe,
that men are stuffed and full to bursting
with their quiet, that this is why they've had to go
into the wilderness, searching for visions
that would deliver up their names. While women
stayed in the villages, with language at their center
like a totem log tipped lengthwise to the ground.
And they chipped at it and picked at it,
making a hole big enough to climb in, a dugout
in which they all paddled off to hunt up
other villages, the other members of the tribe.
And when the men returned they found no one home,
just cold fire pits that would not speak — an old
old forsakenness they bring to the bar stools
while the jukebox music washes over each of them
like a tricolored light wheel on a silver tree.
Though someone might argue that none of whatever

I've just said is true: it was men who made boats
while the women sat clumped in private guilds,
weaving their baskets tight enough to trap
the molecules of water. You can see
that the trail from here to the glove factory
would not be terribly long or hard to read,
and how it might eventually lead to the railroad flat
where, alone at night for many years, my grandmother
works deep into her privacy with a common nail
that she scratches across the backs of copper sheets.
She is making either the hands clasped in prayer
or the three-quarter profile of Jesus.
As far as I know there is nothing
the radio can play now that will make her sing.

Pomegranate

How charitable to call it fruit, when almost nothing
inside it can be eaten. Just the gelatin
that thinly rinds the unpalatable seed.
The rest of it all pith, all bitter,
hardly a meal, even for a thin girl. But food enough,

at least in the myth, to be what ties Persephone
half the year to hell — though it's never clear
this future isn't the one she wants,
her other choice being daylight, sure,
but also living with her mother. In some versions

she willingly eats the tart red seeds, signing on
with the underground gods and their motorbikes
and their dark shades. Oh... all right —
no motorbikes. And "eats" is not right either.
But what, then — "sucks"? "Strains the seeds through her teeth"?

It would have made more sense for Hades to tempt her
with something full of juice: a grapefruit, say,
or peach. But only a girl like Eve
could be so blank a slate as to ruin herself
with a meal as salutary as the apple. Give her instead

the kind of nourishment that takes its own
equipment to extract, like the pomegranate or the spiny
asteroid of the Chinese chestnut. Or the oyster,
from which, between the shell and shucking knife,
there is no exiting unscathed: a *delicacy,* we say,

though the hand hangs out its little flag of skin.
But doesn't the blood that salts the mouth somehow
make the meat taste sweeter? And if she'd turned
toward us in the moonlight with the red pulp
mottling her teeth: wouldn't our innards

have started to sing? I know that's what mine did
those nights when our girl got called out of the junipers
where the rest of us hid her — all it took
was his deep voice, and she stepped out.
Then came sounds that, instead of carrying words,

carried punctuation's weight: the exclamation
when she had the air knocked out, and the question mark
that was her sudden inswept breath.
And the parentheses when time went on forever,
when there was no sound because he'd got her by the throat.

Her boyfriend seemed to like our watching, his imperiousness
lecturing on what we didn't know: the jelly
sluiced inside the mouth or the seeds
rasped across the palate… until it ended sometimes
when he strolled her off, steering

as if she were the boat and her skinny arm
were its tiller. But just as often
he'd have somewhere to get to, or lose interest
as if so much activity had pushed him to the brink of sleep,
and that's how she came back to us kneeling

in our patch of stunted trees, whose evergreenery
pressed its crewelwork in our haunches.
Even by mere moonlight it was hard

not to see the art in what he'd done:
her lip iridescent, her chin gleaming

like the hemisphere of a tarnished spoon.
And didn't the leaves seem brighter then,
if it can be said that junipers have leaves?
As our hard panting rattled through
…but no. Stop here. No of course it can't be said.

Crash Course in Semiotics

1.

"Naked woman surrounded by police": that's one way
to start the poem. But would she mean anything
devoid of her context, in this case a lushly
late-August deciduous forest, some maple,
mostly oak? She carries no prop—for example,
no bike chain, which the cops could be sawing
from the tree trunk that she's wedded to her body.
But let's start with her pure, and untranslated,
as the famous cartoon of the door is a mystery
until we post the word LADIES at a point that would be
four feet up from the ground if this door
were not drawn two inches tall—it's *us*,
you see, who make believe it corresponds
to a "true-life" human door. Does it help
if I say the naked woman is "really" my true-
life friend, she of the tangled dago surname
we don't need to get into here? And if I say next
that she has been swimming — in Lake Tiorati —

2.

you can see how straightaway the tangling subdivides
into (a) where the hell is Lake Tiorati?
and (b) why naked? — to the last let me answer
that it's 1978 and she is twenty; at college
she's been reading Simone de Beauvoir and learning
words like *patriarchy* and *oppression*.
And these have been Mixmastered into her thinking
even about swimsuits — i.e., that not to wear one
is to rip the sign off the door and stomp it

underfoot. When she lies on a rock
the last thing she expects is the tingling
she feels now against her wrist, from a guy
peeing brazenly at her perimeter. This
is an impasse whose bud she thought she had nipped
by aggravating her muscles into interlaced mounds
so her body resembles a relief map of the Appalachians.
In whose northernmost range this story unfolds
& hence the much-delayed answer to item (a), above.

3.

"Naked woman dadadadada police": not a story but words
at the end of a chain whose first link is her realizing
that the Puerto Rican kids across the lake
splashing and whooping are not having fun —
though this is the sign that she'd stuck on their door.
No, there's another word for the kid
slapping his palms on the water:
Drowning. Even the urinater abruptly stops
his stream and stumbles back from her, ashamed.
And because she's the one with the lifeguard build
and because all the guys are much too drunk,
without even thinking she finds herself paddling
toward the spot these kids are now screaming *Julio!* at,
where she draws a mental *X* upon the water.
Of course, it is a fantasy, the correspondence
that would make a drawing equal life, and so
you understand how amazing it is, when she dives
to the bottom and her hand happens on the child.

4.

Perhaps what she expected was for the men on shore
to pay her no mind, as in Manet's *Déjeuner…:*
the naked woman sits among them, yet she is a ghost.
But the kids keep yelling *Julio!* even after
she's hauled the wet one out, the one
she points to: *Julio okay. No,* they shriek,
Julio otro! words she knows just enough Spanish
to know mean there's another Julio in the lake.
Whom she cannot save despite her next round of diving,
which lasts until the cops come hiking down the trail
in their cop shoes. Then she comes ashore
and stands shivering among them, telling the story
calmly enough until she ends it with: for Christ's sake
can't anyone give her a T-shirt? They're staring
as if somehow she's what's to blame, seeing a naked
woman, not the miracle. Which is, of course,
the living boy, that with these words — *Julio otro!* —
we manage to make sense to anyone at all.

Serotonin

Let be be finale of seem.

WALLACE STEVENS

At year's end, the news from here
concerns the new ordinance against couches: no couches
allowed on porches anymore, except for those designed

for outdoor use. The mayor thinks we'll feel better
after the banishment of all that soggy misused foam,
corollary to the gray mood that shall be lifted

like a beached log by the tide. But you know me,
already worrying how to know this outdoor couch
now that a fifty-dollar citation rides on the difference

between velour and vinyl, rattan and wicker,
cushion and mat. Last night was the solstice:
I spent it shivering around a forty-gallon drum whose flame

we party creatures were to feed with slips of paper
inscribed with our woes from this year past.
But I wanted to burn nothing and stood there flummoxed

by my strange absence of regret… until I remembered
the nightly tablets reminiscent of moths, the white
generics the pharmacist swears are the same

as the yellow pills that January started with.
And I do feel better—though humbled, a bit foolish
to figure such heartsickness a matter of ions

merely orbiting a lobe of brain, much like the hydrangea
at the southeast corner of the house, how it becomes
a blue shrub if you bury old nails in its roots. This

I don't get: how one day the tide marsh at sunrise
can make your blood overrun your chest, and the next day
it's just a sweatshop for salt flies, the rain

a thorn nest on your head. Or how the eagle
detendoning a heron carcass
where the Skokomish River has outrun its banks

can be, for my friend up in Canada, just one
more emblem of America's mawkishness & glop.
He calls them shithawks, having seen so many

galumphing bedraggled through the dump, where they slit
the mountain of shiny sacks in search
of undigested grease. And yet it's the same bird

that made me drive into a fence post
while I gawked at the deluged field — amazed,
amazed I ever wanted not to be here. News flash:

what's been walking around in my clothes all these years
turns out to have been a swap meet of carbons
and salts: what can be poured into the ground to make

the hydrangea red again. As the sadness inherent
in a wet clime's winter might just be this same
image thing, a moldy beach ball smell that'll disappear

once we straighten out the business with the couches.
Meanwhile someone tell Wallace Stevens he was wrong about seem:
Seem is good. Seem is everything.

Lament in Good Weather

So would this be how I'd remember my hands
(given the future's collapsing trellis):
pulling a weed (of all possible gestures),
trespassing the shade between toppled stalks?
A whole afternoon I spent chopping them back,
no fruit but a glut of yellow buds, the crop choked
this year by its own abundance, the cages
overrun. And me not fond of tomatoes, really,
something about how when you cut to their hearts
what you find is only a wetness and seeds,
wetness and seeds, wetness and seeds.
Still, my hands came gloved with their odor
into this room, where for days I've searched
but found no words to fit.
Bitter musky acrid stale — the scent
of hands once buried past the wrist in vines.

The Oldest Map with the Name America

1.

In Martin Waldseemüller's woodblock, circa 1507,
the New World is not all there.
We are a coastline
without substance, a thin strip
like a movie set of a frontier town.
So the land is wrong and it is empty
but for one small black bird facing west,
the whole continent outlined with a hard black edge
too strictly geometric, every convolution squared.
In the margin, in a beret, Amerigo Vespucci
pulls apart the sharp legs of his compass —
though it should be noted that instead of a circle
in the Oldest Map with the Name America
the world approximates that shape we call a heart.

2.

The known world once stretched from my house
to the scrim of trees at the street's dead end,
back when the streets dead-ended instead of cleaving
into labyrinths of other streets. I was not
one of those who'd go sailing blithely
past the neighborhood's bright rim:
Saturdays I spent down in the basement
with my Thingmaker and Plastigoop...
Sunday was church, the rest was school,
this was a life, it was enough. Then one day
a weird kid from down the block pushed back
the sidewall of that edge, spooling me

like a fish on the line of his backward walking
fifty yards deep into the woodlot. Which
was barely wild, its trees bearing names
like sugar maple, its snakes being only
garter snakes. Soon the trail funneled
to a single log spanning some unremarkable
dry creek that the kid got on top of,
pointed at and said: You fall down there,
you fall forever. And his saying this
worked a peculiar magic over me: suddenly
the world lay flat and without measure.
So that when I looked down at the dead leaves
covering the ravine they might have
just as well been paint, as depth
became the living juice squeezed out
of space: how far
could you fall? Then the leaves shifted,
their missing third dimension reconfigured
into sound: a murmuring snap
like the breakage of tiny bones that sent me
running back to the world I knew.

3.

Unlike other cartographers of his day,
Waldseemüller wasn't given to ornamenting his maps
with any of Pliny's pseudohuman freaks,
like the race of men having one big foot
that also functions as a parasol.
Most likely he felt such illustrations
would have demeaned the science of his art,
being unverifiable, like the rumored continents
Australia, Antarctica, which he judiciously leaves out.
Thus graced by its absence, the unknown world
floats beyond the reach of being named,

and the cannibals there
don't have to find out yet they're cannibals:
they can just think they're having lunch.

    4.

My point is, he could have been any of us:
with discount jeans and a haircut made
by clippers that his mother ordered
from an ad in a women's magazine.
Nothing off about him except for maybe
how tumultuously the engines that would run
his adult body started up, expressing
their juice in weals that blistered
his jaw's skin as its new bristles
began telescoping out. Stunned
by the warped ukulele that yesterday had been
his predictable voice, the kid
one day on the shortcut home from practice
with the junior varsity wrestling squad
knocked down a little girl in the woods
where what he did was nameless & terrible
& ended with something written on her stomach.
Bic pen, blond girl: the details ran
through us like fire, with a gap
like the eye of the flame where you could
stick your finger and not get burned.
By sundown the whole family slipped,
and the kid's yellow house hulked
empty and dark, with a real estate sign
canted foolishly in its front yard.
Then for weeks our parents went round
making the noise of baby cats
stuck up in trees: who knew? who knew?
We thought they were asking each other

what the kid wrote with the Bic —
what word, what map — and of course
once they learned the answer
they weren't going to say.

5.

In 1516, Martin Waldseemüller
draws another map in which the King of Portugal
rides saddled on a terrifying fish.
Also the name "America"
has been replaced by "Terra Cannibalor,"
with the black bird changed to a little scene
of human limbs dangling from trees
as if they had been put up there by shrikes.
Instead of a skinny strip, we're now
a continent so large we have no back edge,
no westward coast — you could walk left
and wind up off the map. As the weird kid did —
though the world being round, I always half-expect
someday to intersect the final leg of his return.

6.

Here the story rides over its natural edge
with one last ornament to enter in the margin
of its telling. That is, the toolshed
that stood behind the yellow house,
an ordinary house that was cursed
forever by its being fled. On the shed
a padlock bulged like a diamond,
its combination gone with all the other
scrambled numbers in the weird kid's head,
so that finally a policeman had to come
and very theatrically kick the door in
after parking one of our town's two squad cars

with its beacon spinning at the curb.
He took his time to allow us to gather
like witnesses at a pharaoh's tomb,
eager to reconstitute a life
from the relics of its leaving.
And when, on the third kick, the door flopped back
I remember for a moment being blinded
by dust that woofed from the jamb in one
translucent, golden puff. Then
when it settled, amid the garden hose
and rusty tools we saw what all
he'd hidden there, his cache
of stolen library books. Derelict,
lying long unread in piles that sparked
a second generation of anger…
from the public brain, which began to rant
about the public trust. While we
its children balled our fists
around the knot of our betrayal:
no book in the world had an adequate tongue
to name the name of what he did.

   7.

Dying, Tamburlaine said: Give me a map
then let me see how much is left to conquer.
Most were commissioned by wealthy lords,
the study of maps being often prescribed
as a palliative for melancholy.
In the library of a castle of a prince
named Wolfegg, the two Waldseemüller maps
lay brittling for centuries — "lost,"
the way I think of the weird kid as lost
somewhere in America's back forty, where
he could be floating under many names.

One thing for sure, he would be old now.
And here I am charting him: no doubt
I have got him wrong, but still he will be my conquest.

    8.

Sometimes when I'm home we'll go by the house
and I'll say to my folks: come on,
after all these years it's safe
just to say what really happened.
But my mother's mouth will thin exactly
as it did back then, and my father
will tug on his earlobe and call the weird kid
one mysterious piece of work.
In the old days, I assumed
they thought they were protecting me
by holding back some crucial,
devastating piece. But I too am grown
and now if they knew what it was
they'd tell me, I should think.

Home

In Renaissance paintings, it's somewhere apart
from the peopled scene. A somewhere whose trees
grow in spires or in cordial tufts, and each rock
is deliberate, a fragment of the chipped world

washed, tumbled, reset. At least that's what we see
through the window in Ghirlandaio's painting
of the grandfather with his famously warted nose:
the trees and the river horseshoeing toward

the purplish, symmetric butte. A pastoral elsewhere.
Someplace to offset this man and his blebs
buckling one on the next. When we know what's really
outside the window — Florence's open sewers,

beggar-child X and Signor Y's ulcered foot —
after all, this is the fifteenth century, every rat
packing off its plague-fleas to the next new town.
No wonder Ghirlandaio puts that town someplace

the rats could never get to from here, not without
scaling a glacier or paddling through water
whose current would be the weir that strains them out.
Even Saint Sebastian, in frescoes by Mantegna

and Pollaiuolo, becomes foreground to a river
that runs from mountains jacketed in snow.
But lacking shadow, depth… as if to ask us
what good perspective is in dire circumstances,

like here, now, Saint Sebastian with an arrow sticking
through his head. Ghirlandaio, Pollaiuolo —
it took a trip to the library to rekindle the names,
and on my way home to write them down, I stopped

to buy some bread at Bayview Grocery. It's a place
that reminds me of those paintings: something
about how the dust congeals into a yellow varnish
gilding the labels on the cling-peach tins,

but here, outside, the Sound also plunges a foamy arm inland
beside the dumpster. And if you stand at the parking lot's
western edge on cloudless days, you see tall peaks
tinted by distance, with nothing else in the landscape

to match their shades — the purples and salmony orange
and full-blown, flamingo pink almost too
too lavish, as though whatever god made them were running
for a city council seat. Of course

when you get there, the mountains are never purple,
and come evening the mist slides down the couloirs
to settle in the back crease of your neck. But from here
doesn't *there* look romantic, aren't you shanghaied

by its Shangri-La, and don't you start thinking
about the Kennedy administration, doesn't it make you feel
like being kissed? Nearby the city council's commissioned
a concrete man and woman to do just that: kiss

till kingdom come while her knee rises underneath
her dress. It's a civic-minded embrace, though: one woman
and one man oblivious to her breasts, quite different
from what's going on by the pay phone, where one man

grapples with another. Not lovers, their bodies big
with the scent of dead leaves turned. The heavier man
leans back against the ice freezer while the smaller man
kneels before him like a supplicant, their drunkenness

a lifeboat swamped by words. And I hear something
about five dollars missing, which makes the bigger man
take down his pants — to prove what he has, which is nothing
but the lumpy glands pooled in his hand, a gesture

whose earnestness in another context might seem almost
touching. But the friend is touching, isn't touched,
bug-eyed with scrutiny and stern outrage as he pokes
through what is offered like a nest of pale blue eggs

— though *friend* is probably too strong a word
to link these men who only happen to be trapped together
when a pie-piece of the world shears off: my slice
between parking spot and doorway in. Already a woman

is directing traffic away while I stop to look.
My guess is that these guys come from the lean-tos
of corrugated metal scavenged along the chop,
about which there are letters in the paper every day

that go: *How come these lowlifes get to live by the inlet*
while the rest of us have to shell out every month
for crummy solid walls? And they're made out of what —
Sheetrock? Cardboard pancaked with chalk? Ten years ago

I'd have said people live by the inlet because
the human creature, even in its trials, seeks beauty out.
But now I think that come nightfall the beautiful place
is often simply darkest, where if you keep your fire small

the cops aren't likely to come. As it's unlikely
these guys — if they can locate their money —
will find on aisle 6B that good Napa cabernet on sale
before suction-stepping their way back across the mud

to a nice burl of driftwood they'll straddle to drink
and discourse on the astounding chromatograph produced
by the sun's sliding down the back side of the world.
But who am I to say? Me here making another slice

by taking those men and, as we say, "using them,"
using the names I liked best — Mantegna, Ghirlandaio,
Pollaiuolo — though there were so many paintings
of Saint Sebastian's martyrdom to choose from, all

with some place in the background where the river goes
about its business and the hills are ripe with sheep.
Countryside that's lost on Saint Sebastian, who's already
tied up and arrowed through. But it's there

if you need it, if you want to tell yourself
another life is not so far away, just a few days
by donkey. And if, when you get there, the rocks
don't suit your taste, you'll find another landscape

right behind — another mountain, another river
falling one after another like old calendar pages.
Too pretty, their colors too perfect, these places
you would never believe in. But still you would go there.

The Salmon underneath the City

What are they doing down there but unsettling me,
swimming through that seamless dark:
passing into the culvert and under the boat shop,
under the Cadillac dealership with its ghost fins.
Under the backyard, under the parking lot
where milk trucks are bedded down with dogs; at night
electricity floods the wires above the chain-link.

And sometimes I study the garden's broken dirt
to detect the groundswell of their passage.
Or I walk out to the cedars where the culvert
feeds them back to Moxlie Creek. But so far,
nothing. Except one I saw leap
from the water in a perfect, frizzled crescent,
there where the stub of silver pipe ungutters

in the bay. The guy who'd hooked it
showed me the telltale black gums in its mouth,
after I'd watched him palm a rock and bring it down
hard on the skull, watched the fish relinquish
then sigh all its living out. That was weeks ago
and ever since I've listened for the wilderness
they make of their compulsion, of their one idea:

Against. Under the milk yard, where the dogs' chops
quiver, and the wires sing with what moves through
and makes them full (on rainy nights,
even the hardware glistens). And sometimes I find myself
stalled under a streetlamp, snagged by the curb
like a yellow leaf. Crouched there to look
where a storm grate opens over these dark waters.

The Ghost Shirt

Museum of Natural History, NYC, 5/1/92, the first day of the riots

The blue whale swam through blue air in the basement
while upstairs the elephants twined together tusk by tusk,
and the enormous canoe was being rowed by the Tlingit

as they have rowed without moving for years through the dusk
in the Hall of the Americas. Empty space
was brocaded by schoolkids' shrieks

as teachers pantomimed in front of each glass case,
and I turned a corner and came up smack against the ghost shirt
worn by a mannequin with no legs and no face —

                                                  at first
it almost didn't register;
it was not what books had led me to expect: no beads
no ornament no chamois leather

or those shiny cornets made from rolled-up snuff-tin lids.
Instead it was just a cotton shift
negotiating grimly between blue and green and red,

with some glyphs scrawled amateurishly across the breast
in ordinary pen: a thunderbird and some lightning,
a buffalo and a hoofprint,

one tree, one little man puffing
on a flume-size pipe. Pentagram stars formed a cloud
atopside a smaller species of stippling

that I had to stare at a long time before I understood
meant bullets. Then I found myself checking for broken threads
to see if any of the holes were rimmed in blood —

but no: time or moths or bullets, it was anybody's guess.
A quote on the wall from the Paiute messiah
said *Indians who don't believe in the ghost dance*

will grow little, just about a foot high,
and stay that way. Then some of those
will be turned into wood and burned in fire —

and I left the museum wondering about which was worse:
to display a man's blood here
so every kid can practice crumpling as if falling off a horse

(& the kid knows exactly how to clutch the new air
entering his heart). Or to clean the shirt
as if the ghost blood had never been there.

    ◆ ◆ ◆

This is the kind of story you could carry around
like a beaded keychain from a tourist trap:
how the ghost dance became a thunderstorm
that even summoning Buffalo Bill out
to the Standing Rock agency could not slake —
until the schoolhouses were empty
and the trading stores were empty
and the winter wheat went bony in the field
and the War Department had no idea what it meant
but that the Sioux had gone mad with their dancing
and that Yellow Bird wore a peculiar shirt when he chanted
Your bullets will not go toward us right before they did.

    ◆ ◆ ◆

From the museum, I take the subway downtown
and change trains where the tunnels all converge
below Times Square, in one dank cavern underground

whose darkness seems so large it does not have edges.
Even at midafternoon, the shade there seethes
with people marching in a lockstep through that passage;

sometimes, when directed back over a shoulder, a mouth
on someone's profiled face will drop
and I'll see the tongue dart nervously along the teeth…

then the march becomes a gallop
when the walls begin to pound with an arriving train,
its riders rushing toward us in a yellowness crushed up

against the glass. And we board like cattle, one person
driving an elbow into another's gut
as we jam in (and we jam in…)

and coming up at Grand Central, I find it likewise knotted
with people ranged in single-files,
shuffling toward the ticket counters in fits and stops

that give them time to paw the vast floor with their heels.
But what strikes me most is how loudly the silence
murmurs off the marble tiles

as if we were all underwater, hearing backward our own breath.
Then I remember that I bought a return on my way in
and hurry back down two flights of steps

to the lower level, where the train for Croton
sits almost full, though not scheduled to leave for half an hour
yet. Soon all the seats are gone

but the train keeps filling, arms and legs the mortar
in a wall of breasts and double-breasts. I avoid the gaze
and glare of those who hang on straps over

my head, and it isn't until the train begins to wheeze
from its hydraulics and slowly labors
past the gate that everyone around me will unfreeze

enough to speak: about a city bus and its passengers
rocked onto its flank and set aflame, a hundred black
and Spanish kids aswarm with Molotovs and crowbars…

which is the story we sow along the darkness, until the track
rises into daylight above Ninety-Seventh Street,
where the broken windows have been boarded back

with plywood, each painted with its own domestic scene
— curtains gathered primly or potted geraniums on the sills —
though otherwise, everything looks to me as it has always been,

with the same nimbuses of spray paint on the trestles,
the alphabet stuffed like heavy furniture
reciting its addition on the same brick walls

…until we cross the East River
where everybody lets their breath go with relief,
the wheels droning their steady whuckerwhuckerwhucker

as the train settles into its top speed
and we skitter along the Hudson, where nothing is except
water on one side, on the other side a ravine

overstudded with junk: a Cadillac sunk axle-
deep a shopping cart the front wheels of a stroller
menacingly airborne like the forelegs of *Tyrannosaurus rex* —

and it's here the train zippers
to an abrupt stop (though we haven't come to any station),
steeping us anxiously awhile in quiet, until the whispers

blossom like umbrellas opening before the rain:
first *they're blocking the engine* then *they're lying down
on the tracks,* rumors that ripple through the train

like a wave sweeping upstream, then back down,
by which time the muttering has escalated to a shout
that goes *Keep going!* and *We've got to run those fuckers down!*

⁘

Between the train and whoever lies down in its path,
you could say there's a ghost shirt,
whatever it is that makes the locomotive stop
if the engineer can see far enough ahead.
I think it is a dotted line
looping the outskirts of our being human —
ghostly because of the ease with which
its perforations can be ripped. Also
because the sole proof of its presence
lies in the number of days we go unhurt,
a staggering number, especially when you consider
how much bigger the world is than a train.

And how something even as small as a bullet
can pick out of elsewhere's 359 degrees
one shape, and suddenly everything is changed,
though the calx of what didn't happen
remains in curiously enduring traces
like the stone casts that larval caddis flies
leave behind them in the stream
(& *larva:* from the Latin word for ghost).
What you have is always less
a history of a people, any people,
than a history of its rocks: first a heap
then a cathedral and soon a heap again,
while the names get amortized like money.
Like Damian Williams, the one they called Football,
who held his bloody cinderblock aloft
and danced as if he were stomping out a hundred
baby flames: Rodney King, Reginald Denny,
William Cody, Stacey Koon. And Black Coyote,
who refused to give up his Winchester
after Yellow Bird danced the first few steps
before Colonel Forsyth's pony soldiers
broke all hell loose. And Black Coyote,
who Turning Hawk said was crazy,
"a young man of very bad influence and in fact a nobody."

                    ◆ ◆ ◆

I want to say that we all weren't white on that train,
but mostly we were —
and when without explanation the engine started up again,

those who weren't fell away to the edge of the herd
and got off where the conductor squawked out *Spuyten Duyvil,*
Marble Hill and *Yonkers*…

and as we rolled I strained to imagine the sound a wheel
would make as it milled through someone's ribs,
listening for them bedded down in every mile

until I got off way out in the suburbs.
From the station I called my father to come pick me up
and waited for him half-hidden in some shrubs

so that when he arrived I could make my usual leap
into his Mercedes so no one sees me getting in.
I remember what it was like in that town, growing up

so out of it I didn't even see the affluence back then —
and how we kids rolled our eyes whenever our parents
started in on the WPA and the Great Depression

and being glad for a day's honest work even if that meant
no more than laying a stone and piling another on top
— part of a war we waged in serial installments,

mostly over what we put on our backs, or feet, or not:
the tattered clothes we wore to ape a poverty
about which our folks claimed we did not know shit

(though like every kid in that town I toted around my copy
of a gospel that one week was *Soul on Ice*
and the next week *Bury My Heart at Wounded Knee*)

— which maybe explains why it still makes me nervous,
though twenty years have passed: to be riding around in a car
that cost more than, elsewhere, someone's house,

while I'm trying to explain to my old father
what it meant to me to see the ghost shirt
just before Wall Street shut down and every broker

fled. And not just fled, but reverted,
as if what made us human had only been a temporary crust
on our skins, as if there were no way to stop the backward

march into the swamp. Pretty soon we'd all be just
like rats but bigger, and combat ready...
but here again my father claimed I didn't know whereof

I spoke: all day the television had showed the city
eerily at peace. And the only fires were the tiny flames
of candles people held, outside the public library.

from

Luck Is Luck

(2005)

The man who has fed the chicken every day throughout its
life at last wrings its neck instead, showing that more refined
views as to the uniformity of nature would have been useful to
the chicken.

BERTRAND RUSSELL

To My Big Nose

Hard to believe there were actual years
when I planned to have you cut from my face —
hard to imagine what the world would have looked like
if not seen through your pink shadow.
You who are built from random parts
like a mythical creature — a gryphon or sphinx —
with the cartilage ball attached to your tip
and the plaque where the bone flares at the bridge
like a snake who has swallowed a small coin.
Seabird beak or tanker prow
with Modigliani nostrils, like those strolled out
from the dank studio and its close air,
with a *swish swish* whisper from the nude's silk robe
as it parts and then falls shut again.
Then you're out on the sidewalk of Montparnasse
with its fumes of tulips and clotted cream
and clotted lungs and cigars and sewers —
even fumes from the lobster who walks on a leash.
And did his owner march slowly
or drag his swimmerets briskly along
through the one man's Parisian dogturd that is
the other man's cutting-edge conceptual art?
So long twentieth century, my Pygmalion.
So long rhinoplasty and the tummy tuck.
Let the vowels squeak through my sinus-vault,
like wet sheets hauled on a laundry line's rusty wheels.
Oh I am not so dumb as people have made me out,
what with your detours when I speak,
and you are not so cruel, though you frightened men off,
all those years when I thought I was running the show,

pale ghost who has led me like a knife
continually slicing the future stepped into,
oh rudder/wing flap/daggerboard, my whole life
turning me this way and that.

Languedoc

Southern France, the troubadour age:
all these men running around in frilly sleeves.
Each is looking for a woman he could write a song about —
or the moonlight a woman, the red wine a woman,
there is even a woman called the Albigensian Crusade.
It's the tail end of the Dark Age
but if we wait a little longer it'll be the Renaissance
and the forms of the songs will be named and writ down;
wait: here comes the villanelle, whistling along the pike,
repeating the same words over and over
until I'm afraid my patience with your serenade
runs out: time's up. Long ago
I might have been attracted by your tights and pantaloons,
but now they just look silly, ditto for your instrument
that looks like a gourd with strings attached
(the problem is always the strings attached).
Langue d'oc, meaning the language of yes, as in
"Do you love me?" *Oc.* "Even when compared
to her who sports the nipple ring?" *Oc oc.*
"Will we age gracefully and die appealing deaths?"
Oc oc oc oc.
So much affirmation ends up sounding like
a murder of crows passing overhead
and it is easy to be afraid of murder-by-crow —
though sometimes you have to start flapping your arms
and follow them. And fly to somewhere the signs say:
Yes Trespassing, Yes Smoking,
Yes Alcohol Allowed on Premises, Yes Shirt Yes Shoes
Yes Service Yes. Yes Loitering
here by this rocky coast whose waves are small

and will not break your neck; this ain't no ocean, baby,
this is just the sea. Yes Swimming
Yes Bicycles Yes to Nude Sunbathing All Around,
Yes to Herniated Bathing-Cappèd Veterans of World War One
and Yes to Leathery Old Lady Joggers.
Yes to their sun visors and varicose veins in back of their knees,
I guess James Joyce did get here first —
sometimes the Europeans seem much more advanced.
But you can't go through life regretting what you are,
yes, I'm talking to you in the baseball cap,
I'm singing this country-western song that goes: Yeah!
Oc! Yes! *Oui!* We! — will dive — right — in.

The Crows Start Demanding Royalties

Of all the birds, they are the ones
who mind their being armless most:
witness how, when they walk, their heads jerk
back and forth like rifle bolts.
How they heave their shoulders into each stride
as if they hope that by some chance
new bones there would come popping out
with a boxing glove on the end of each.

Little Elvises, the hairdo slicked
with too much grease, they convene on my lawn
to strategize for their class-action suit.
Flight they would trade in a New York minute
for a black muscle-car and a fist on the shift
at any stale green light. But here in my yard
by the Jack in the Box dumpster
they can only fossick in the grass for remnants

of the world's stale buns. And this
despite all the crow poems that have been written
because men like to see themselves as crows
(the head-jerk performed in the rearview mirror,
the dark brow commanding the rainy weather).
So I think I know how they must feel:
ripped off, shook-down, taken to the cleaners.
What they'd like to do now is smash a phone against a wall.
But they can't, so each one flies to a bare branch and screams.

On the Destruction of the *Mir*

Every night space junk falls from the sky—
usually a titanium fuel tank. Usually falling
into the ocean, or into nowhere in particular
because ours is a planet of great vacancies,
no matter how much fog would be required
in downtown Tokyo. In the Skylab days
you'd see people on the streets wearing iron
helmets, like centurions. But nowadays
we go bareheaded, as if to say to the heavens:
Wake me when I am someone else.
Like the man whose car made fast acquaintance
with what Yeats would have called the bole of a tree.
And who now believes he has written
many of the latest hits, which he will sing
for you while he splits a cord of wood:
like a virgin—*whap!*—like a virgin—*whap!*—
until he's got enough fuel for the winter
and a million dollars stashed in an offshore bank.
You may think it's tragic, like my Buddhist friend
who claims that any existence means suffering,
though my gay friend says, *Phooey, what about
Oscar night, what about making popcorn
and wrapping up with your sweetie
in that afghan your great-aunt made so long ago?*
You don't have to dwell on the fact that she's dead
or bring up her last unkempt year in the home,
when she'd ask anyone who walked in the door
to give her a good clunk on the head. Instead,
what about her crocheting these squares
in preposterous colors, orange and green,

though why must their clashing be brought to the fore
if the yarn was enough to keep her happy?
In fact, don't the clashes light the sparks
in this otherwise corny thing? Which is safer
to make than a hole in the skull to let out
the off-gassing of one's bad spirits.
As in trepanation performed by the Incas,
who traded their melancholy for a helmet
made from a turtle shell. You never know
when your brain will require such armor —
could happen sometime when you least expect.
Could even happen when you are parked
behind your desk, where a very loud thump
makes you look up to discover a robin
diving into the window again and again.
It is spring, after all, and in its reflection
the bird may have found the perfect mate:
thus doth desire propel us headlong
toward the smash. Don't even try
translating glass into bird-speak; it only knows
it wants the one who dropped from sight.
Same one who beaned it, same one who's perched,
glaring back from a bough of the Japanese maple
with its breast fit to burst. And behind the lace
of new leaves, there's a wallpaper of clouds —
weighing hundreds of tons
but which float nonetheless —
in the blue sky that seemed to fit so well
when we first strapped it on our heads.

Le deuxième sexe

The famous Polish poet calls Simone de Beauvoir a Nazi hag
but to me she will always be her famous book,
the one with the Matisse paper cut on the cover,
a sad blue nude I took into the woods.
Where we college girls went to coax the big picture
from her, as if she could tell us how to use
all the strange blades on our Swiss Army knives —
the firewood we arranged in either log cabin or tepee,
a little house built to be burned down.
Which could be a metaphor:
Simone as the wind puffing the damp flames,
a cloud with a mouth that became obsolete
once we started using gasoline. Still,
she gave me one lesson that sticks, which is:
do not take a paperback camping in the rain
or it may swell to many times its original size,
and if you start with a big book you'll end up
with a cinderblock. In that vein I pictured Simone as huge
until (much later) I read that her size was near-midget —
imagine, if we took Gertrude Stein, we'd be there still,
trying to build some kind of travois to drag her body out.
The other thing I remember, a word, *immanence* —
meaning, you get stuck with the cooking and laundry
while the man gets to hit on all your friends in Paris.
Sure you can put the wet book in the oven
and try baking it like a cake. But the seam will stay soggy
even when the pages rise, ruffled like French pastry.
As far as laundry goes, it's best I steer clear,
what with my tendency to forget the tissues
wadded in my sleeves. What happens is

I think I'm being so careful, and everything
still comes out like the clearing where we woke.
Covered in flakes that were then the real thing:
snow. Which sounds more la-di-da in French.
But then the sun came up and all *la neige* vanished
like those chapters we grew bored with and had skipped.

The Floating Rib

Because a woman had eaten something
when a man told her not to. Because the man
who told her not to had made her
from another man's bone. That's why
men badgered the heart side of her chest,
knowing she could not give the bone back, knowing
she would always owe them that one bone.

And you could see how older girls who knew
their catechism armed themselves against it:
with the pike end of teasing combs
scabbarded in pocketbooks that clashed
against the regulation jumper's night-watch plaid.
In the girls' bathroom mirror, you watched them
hazard the spike at the edge of their eyes,

shepherding bangs through which they peered
like cheetahs in an upside-downward–growing grass.
Then they'd mouth the words to "Runaway"
and run white lipstick around their lips —
white to announce they had no blood
so any wound would leave no trace, as Eve's
having nothing more to lose must have made her

fearless. What was weird was how soon
the ordinary days started running past them
like a river, and how willingly they entered it
and how they rose up on the other side. Tamed,
or — God, no — your *mother*: ready to settle
with whoever found the bone under her blouse
and give it over, and make a life out of getting it back.

Original Sin

When first they told me the serpent *beguiled* her
I pictured her eyes knocked loose and rattling round
like the gizmo you'd take with you into the closet
and pump with your thumb to make red and blue sparks.
You needed the darkness. You needed the quiet.
You needed the whisper of sleeves on your cheeks.
Most, you needed the shelf where your father's brown hats
squatted like toads, forget about sparks —
the mouth, not the eye, is the holy portal.
Hats with cool satin bellies and stained satin bands
that I put to my tongue when alone in their dark,
compelled by the mystery of his old sweat.
And this much I knew: such an outlaw rite
would command adult fury in the open. You could not
speak of sucking the hats' bowls to your face,
or of licking the grosgrain of their sweat-darkened ribbons:
there was no way to explain why you even wanted this.
Let them think I was in there fooling with my Black Cat sparker
and not tasting the wax that came out of his ears,
not hungry for everything about him that was forbidden.
God cursed the snake — *Thou shalt eat nothing but dust —*
but wasn't Snake a scapegoat for the wrong
that God Himself had done? To name
out of all paradise the one thing denied her,
so Eve would spend those first days walking round
with *apple apple* filling hours in her head?
Sour, sweet — how it tasted went unsaid. Either way,
I doubt the fruit lived up to what she would expect.

The Cardinal's Nephews

They started out like the rest of us, huns
of the vacant fields behind the houses,
where our arrows punctured ancient mattresses
that wobbled drunkenly amid the asters.
It wounded me to think about the cardinal's brother
fornicating even once for each of all his sons,
but when they tied me in the staghorns
and ran their Matchbox cars over my feet, suddenly
it was me too swooning with that fervor to breed an empire.

Then their hair grew out like jigsaw pieces as the decade
kinked and snaked… until it was Saturday night
in small-town downtown, all of them piled
like marsupials in the backseat's pouch. Their car
would be hawing at the curbside while the eldest
bopped into the liquor store for some Wild Irish Rose,
his strides filigreed with a little hiccup
every time he shucked the ballast of his Dingo boot.
Later, when they passed out where the rumpus rooms

gave way between the speakers, or when their car
barreled into the lone tree that stood its ground,
I saw how power suffered its ignominies
without blustering or braking—think of Cesare Borgia
leading the cathedral's *Christ Have Mercies*
in a tin mask after syphilis wrecked his face.
These were the ghosts of men who stood at the altar
wearing spurs and daggers underneath their pleats,
Romans come back now all leather fringe and eyelids

drooping in a rogue half-sleep. The miracle
was how by Sunday Mass their mother always
righted them again. And bullied their hair
into nests like squirrels made, and strapped their neckties
tight to hold up their heads. Then came the rumbling
that was their singing, before the uncle's name
drew through us like a knife, the uncle whose red cap
meant willingness to shed blood for the faith,
though at the time all I knew was its astonishing color.

White Bird/Black Drop

1.

The snowy egret's not extinct
no matter how archaic it may seem:
its crest a rack of spiky feathers
that would ornament a woman's hat
in another era. A less functional era.
Where the hat would go with a backless gown
showing off the woman's spine,
her legs hidden under fabric folds
made sumptuous by light.
We imagine her legs have grace
when in fact they could be sticks,
like the stick legs of the snowy egret,
which are covered in black chitin
that erupts into bright-yellow feet.
Lavishness where it makes no sense,
buried in the mud. So Audubon
painted the bird on shore, giving
the legs the illusion of movement —
& I don't understand: how the feet can lift
when the legs appear to have no meat in them
at all. Their carcasses
littered the park where I worked,
where the birds flew into power lines
that sliced across the marshes.
The legs took only a day in the sun
before becoming dry enough
to be set out in the nature center,
in a box where children stuck their hands
before they looked — a game

about what we imagine from forms that go unseen.
But before too long the legs were banished,
after a woman complained that her son
had been tricked into touching a dead thing
& could not be consoled for weeks.

2.

Now the era wants us working
in order to improve ourselves:
forget Coleridge wandering the upland
stoned out of his head, forget him
& his years in the spare bedroom
at the surgeon Gillman's house
where Gillman doled the Black Drop out
to every day's white page.
The Black Drop, cottage industry of widows:
opium dissolved in quince fruit juice—
& is it wrong to lament its passing
along with extinct words like *quince fruit juice*?
But the snowy egret's not extinct, no matter
how dead it sounds that it should be.
For that you can thank the functional era
for having no patience with ornament:
so women give up fancy hats
& the birds return to the wayside marsh,
where they dot the green like clots of foam
bobbing among the empty bottles.
Once when she was really flying
my girlfriend bought a velvet hat,
a black pillbox with one white plume
shooting straight up from the forehead.
This she wore with rubber boots
to bang on my door at ten p.m.,
my friend plotched on cough syrup,

her mind wandering the upland.
Now that she's dried out,
she fears for her liver; sometimes
(pressing the phone to it) she'll ask,
long-distance, what I think (she thinks
the hat got left on a Greyhound bus).
I think, *Yeah, but remember the fun*
we had walking the stiff plumes of our hair
through fresh snow glowing lilac in the moonlight?
But she says no; those nights were tragic
& she can't remember anything.

3.

Those years my friend gave to Robitussin
I spent chasing after men on bikes,
the loud machines they wore as ornaments
between their legs. They all had the long
black-clad legs of the egret —
spread, slightly bent, from the low-slung seat
& I would have liked to have been one myself
but part of me wanted to stay in the bed,
my spine a white curl replicating
the S-curves of the canyon road,
my plumage perhaps a camisole
with one torn strap. But the choice was either
him or her, looker or looked-at,
subject or object, you could not be both
& me being pigeon-toed & flighty, unable
to hold anything upright with my bad legs…
well, it figures I'd come to land here
where the cedars drip into Ellis Cove
& the long-legged birds stand stock-still
on the stumps: that's how they disguise themselves.
As I'm likewise disguised in a porkpie hat,

binoculars my only ornament besides the clear drop
clinging to the bulb of my nose-tip.
Above the cove, the shoreline road
hugs the curl of the embankment
& the guys (who would be geezers now)
rumble along it on their Honda Gold Wings.

4.

Audubon's most famous painting
I must have looked at a hundred times
before I noticed the tiny hunter
approaching from across the marsh.
Meanwhile the bird keeps the black drop of its eye
steady on us, terrifyingly steady,
as if he accepts this one long moment —
Perfect Beauty — for whatever comes next.
Isn't that why the guys all lit out
on their bikes: to stop time
while they were still in their best feathers?
Shaggy at the head and neck,
they let the whole world enter them —
the speed, the green, the trash-strewn marsh —
looker & looked-at blurred into one thing.
One time when I asked the bad-boy poet
to read his poem about the egret, which I love,
it was not his refusal that angered me
so much as the way that he'd aged
so much better than I had. Now that he's dead
sometimes I'll spot a beauty like his
riding crosstown on the stuttering bus,
like Coleridge on the deck of the *Speedwell*,
sailing toward Malta in his sealskin coat,
though in this case of course it's a black leather jacket,
one of those portable black caves of sleep.

Look at him dozing, hunched into his collar.
Look at him hunched into his wrecked good looks.
If he looks out the window, I bet what he'll notice
is the sky's bearing down now, as if it might snow.
The crushed cans singing in the ditches
& the trash bags pinned to the cyclone fence.
But he won't see the bird
in its grand bright whiteness —
hunkered like a foam-clot, luffing in the wind.

    5.

Getting back, at last, to the salt marsh where I worked:
in the California summers, botulism
rampaged through the ponds.
It made the birds' necks fold
& their long legs double up
as they dragged their shaggy haunches
through the shoreline's stinking dust.
The snowy egret I found
was long past hope — whenever
I found a sick bird on the trail
I was supposed to take it back to the office
where one of the men would break its neck
to keep the disease from spreading.
All right, then. That's what I'd do.
I carried the egret clamped under my arm,
because I'd read that given a chance
it might spear me in the eye
with its black beak. Strange
how it knew the eyeball was soft
& crucial to its being seen, & knew
how the viewer produces the viewed
in a miracle of transference.
Black drop inside of yellow drop,

black drop inside of bluish-gray:
we studied each other while the trapped head twitched.
By the time I got back
all the men had gone home, so I killed the bird
the way they did, by taking its head
in the cave of my hand & making my thumb
& forefinger a collar around its neck.
Then I spun the body until it went limp —
this was easier than I expected.
The late sun was broadcasting
gold light on the marsh, & I did not think of Coleridge
& what the dead bird meant to him.
Instead, in that moment, I felt like a man,
or how I imagined a man might feel.
A delusion, of course, & soon the sun closed shop,
& then all I felt was sadness
for what the world had made of me.

after Larry Levis

On the High Suicide Rate of Dentists

It's no surprise, when you think about what the teeth
are the ramparts of: slippery slope
leading to the gullet. Little jagged-edged ivory
makers of sameness, the Bolsheviks of the dining room:

take the lobster tail or the prime rib,
put in your mouth and chew them awhile
and all class distinctions — whether deep-fried or drowning in butter —
quickly become moot. But any actual tears

are hard drops to explain, especially coming from someone
like the one who played "novelty music"
when he chopped the fillings out of me.
Guitarzan. How lighthearted he seemed

as he chimed along with Jane's falsetto yodeling.
And though you might think gastroenterologists
would wear the crown of their despairs,
at least they witness how bygones can be bygones

and how the burden can be released. Versus this
perpetual going-in, which is always the scariest part
of the story: *Give up hope, all ye who enter here.*
Even the radishes are doomed, cut so painstakingly into roses.

So maybe part of their sadness comes from the sushi
assembled to look like the stained glass at Chartres.
Or the crown roast whose bones wear those paperboy caps
while ever so eager the knife goes in.

Freshwater and Salt

When we were young girls and swam naked in Turkey Lake
we were like animals: our legs were thickly furred.
We took the trees' rustling for a sign of their watching.
Even the limestone drooled from its mouth cracks.

But then I got real: it was only lake ledges, dripping—
rainwater, sweat of moss, and dew.
Maybe a man hid behind a birch's pale skin
and I saw him, once. The rest, my ego running wild.

Still, it's the roundabout way that I'm taking to the island
that is Indian land, where I lie down without my shirt.
This is years from the lake, and the water is salt
when a rockslide clatters off the bluff.

Make the clatter a sign of the watchers come forward—
in the calm that comes after, I can hear their feet.
But the trees have long since surrendered their trench coats
and gone back to being simple trees.

First thought, *I've grown old*; second thought is the cops,
but I keep my eyes closed to stall their skirmish
over me. Time clicks like their footsteps as they come close—
until a musty breath whelms down my face.

Now hold it there, freeze-frame, while I look up
at the sun's corona on a mule deer's chin.
Chewing some fox grass, regarding me only
because on this wild shore I am strange.

In the Confessional Mode, with a Borrowed Movie Trope

…and then there is the idea of another life
of which this outward life is only an expression,
the way the bag floating round in the alley
traces out the shape of wind
but is not wind. In a fleabag hotel
in Worcester, Mass., a man is dying,
muscles stiff, their ropes pulled taut,
his voice somewhere between a honk and whisper.
But float down through the years, many years,
and it's us, meaning me and the man
as a boy upstairs in the house
where I've finagled my deflowering.
Maybe finagled. Hard to say if it's working.
It reminds me of trying to cram a washrag
down a bottle neck — you twist and twist
to make it reach, but it does not,
and in the end the inside of me
was not wiped clean. Oh I was once
in such a hurry. The job had to be done
before the pot roast was, his stepmother
thumping the ceiling under us: *Whatever
you're doing, you better get out
of your sister's room.* But her voice
carried more of the wasp's irritation
than the hornet's true rage, so we forged on —
while our jury of trusty busty Barbies
perched on their toes, their gowns iridescent,
a sword of gray light coming through the curtain crack
and knighting me where I contorted
on the rug. And it's clear to me still,

what I wanted back then; namely, my old life
cut up into shreds so I could get on
with my next. But the boy was only
halfway hard, no knife-edge there,
though the rest of him looked as if it were bronze,
with muscles rumpling his dark-gold skin.
Meaning this is a story about beauty after all.
And when the roast was ready, I slipped outside,
where November dusk was already sifting down
into the ballrooms underneath the trees.
It was time to go home to my own dinner,
the ziti, the meatballs, *Star Trek* on TV,
but how could I sit there, familiar among them,
now that I was this completely different thing?
Sweat was my coat as I flew from his house
while the brakes of my ten-speed sang like geese.
But now it's his voice that resembles a honk
in a room where the empty amber vials
rattle underneath his narrow bed. Meaning
he's trying hard to take himself out.
And while I have as yet no theory
to unlock the secret forces of the earth, still
I think there's a reason why the boy and I,
when we grew up, both got stuck
with the same disease. Meaning the stiffness,
the spasms, the concrete legs —
oh I was once in such a hurry. Now
my thighs are purple from all the drugs
I'm shooting in, & I don't even want to know
how the boy looks racked and wrecked.
Sometimes in the midst of making love
that kind of body will come floating in,
but quickly I'll nudge it away in favor of
the airbrushed visions. But not him,

the young him, the brass plate of whose belly
would be more lovely than I could bear,
though in chaster moments I will visit
that alcove of me where his torso is struck
by all the dark-gold light that still slants in.
Oh we are blown, we are bags,
we are moved by such elegant chaos.
Call it god. Only because it is an expletive that fits.
His body, his beauty, all fucked up now.
God. Then the air cuts out, and then we drop.

Fubar

for Paul Guest

For starters, scratch the woman weeping over her dead cat —
sorry, but pet death barely puts the needle in the red zone.
And forget about getting brownie points
for any heartbreak mediated by the jukebox.
See the leaves falling: isn't this the trees' way of telling us to just buck up?

Oh they are right: their damage is so much greater than our damage.
I mean, none of my body parts have actually dropped off.
And when the moon is fat and handsome, I know we should be grateful
that its face is only metaphor; it has no teeth to chew us out.
In fact, the meadow isn't spattered with the tatters of our guts.

But in last night's hypnagogic dreamscape where I went
to collect some data. Where I was just getting into the swing of things
tranquillity-wise. Then this kid came rolling through the moonlight
in a bed with lots of Rube Goldberg traction rigging.
And it was a kid like you, some kid with a broken neck.

And maybe beauty is medicine quivering on the spoon
but surely you have noticed — the calf painted on the famous old Greek urn
is headed to the slaughter. And don't get me started
on the wildflowers or they will lead me to the killer bees.
And that big ol' moon will lead to a cross section of the spinal cord.

And the trees to their leaves, all smushed in the gutter.
And the gutter to the cat squashed flat as a hotcake.
And the hotcake to the grits, and the grits to the South,
where the meadows were once battlefields.
Where a full moon only meant a better chance of being shot.

But come on, the sun is rising, I'll put a bandage on my head,
and we'll be like those guys at the end of the movie —
you take this crutch made from a stick.
For you the South is a mess, what with its cinders and its smoldering.
And lookee, lookee here at me: I'm playing the piccolo.

from *Luck Is Luck*

Bulletin from Somewhere up the Creek

Luckily, it's shallow enough that I can pole my rubber boat —
don't ask what happened to the paddle. Anywhere is lovely
if you look hard enough: the scum on the surface
becomes a lace of tiny flowers.
In the space between cedars, a half-moon slides
across a sky colored like the inside of a clam.
Two terns slice it with their sharp beaks,
gape-mouthed and wheeling and screaming like cats.

See, nature is angry, I said to myself: *Nature
is just an ice pick with wings.* Then a weasel or something
poked its head through the muck, looked around for a while
before submerging again. And not even bumping
the ketchup squeeze bottle seemed to disturb it,
nor was it afraid to lose itself in this brown soup.
Or maybe this was just a very large rat — still,
why should its example be of any less worth?

Ah, my friends, I could tell you my troubles
but is that why you came? Sure, it stinks here —
the best birding is done in foul-smelling places.
So far I've seen the hawk circling, the kingfisher chuckling
before smashing itself breast-first into the muck.
I've watched the blue heron standing on just one leg
until it found something half-rotten to spear. Then swallowing
with a toss of its head, as if this were a meal for kings.

Urban Legend

Like many stories, this one begins with Jesus —
well, he sure looks like Jesus, this guy pulled over by the ditch.
Let's say the tarp has blown off the back of his Isuzu pickup.
Let's say that the apostles are slowly rising heavenward.

See them twisting in the thermals, in this sky that's not a joke
even if these fugitives could figure in a gag's protracted setup.
Calling for the hauling of twelve helium-filled desire dolls —
to a toga party. See how the apostles all have boners underneath their robes.

And isn't that like me, to put the *boners* into play,
however inappropriate, when this is not a joke.
This is not a joke because the story wants to go into the record.
Yes, it does want. The story has a little mind that thinks.

And the mind sends its ambassadors: these poodles nuked in microwaves,
bonsai kittens, sewer crocodiles, rats suckled in maternity wards.
I believe in the fatal hairdo just for the love of saying *fatal hairdo*.
And I believe in the stolen kidney because I too have woken up with something missing.

But I haven't spoken yet of the rapture, another word whose saying
is like dancing at a toga party after downing many shots.
Because who hasn't tried to pull their arms from the sleeves of gravity's lead coat?
Who doesn't have at least one pair of wax wings out in the garage?

So back to Jesus, back to daylight, and you can make the dimwit me
who launches herself into the updraft of the rapture
and goes sailing straight through the story's sunroof. Above, the bonsai kittens
pad the sky as cherubim. Below me, hairdos right and left are going up in smoke.

Now the apostles are storming heaven, the Isuzu's motor's ticking,
while the left hand of Jesus forms a ledge above his brow.
And you, Earth angel, fear not my crash landing in the diamond lane —
the vinyl men are full of noble gas, and I'm rising on my balsa wings.

A Simple Camp Song

In the days of yore, three handsome drunks
took me to sea until my jigging hook was swallowed.
I reeled its line around a plywood chock
until the big fish hovered at the ceiling of the water.

I know this sounds like a fable, so let it be a fable
in the rain where we hunched underneath our stupid hats.
We didn't have a gun, so one of the drunks leaned out
and drove a gaffing hook under its jawbone.

A loud *whump* from the transom when the rope played out;
then the little boat stood on its hind end. We rose up
with the bench seats pinned behind our knees
and hung in the air until the boat sat down again.

And nobody's lungs were inundated by the sea
in this soft-core, cloud-upholstered version of the past.
Someone merely pulled the starter and we towed the fish to shore,
where it sprawled on the wet sand, bigger than a woman.

I know a fable would have coughed up a pearl or a word
but the fish was a fish, lying there, not speaking.
Its lips did move in a mockery of speech,
its gills a set of louvers, opening and closing.

Then the drunks found sticks and I did, too,
and we brought them down on the shovel of its skull.
But the fish wouldn't die until I put some weight behind the stick,
until I jumped with my upswing, like a primitive.

Buh went the stick. It felt all right to be barbaric,
to be cut from the same cloth as the wilderness itself.
But soon a birding group appeared on the bluff
and stripped all the teeth off the gears inside their lungs.

The drunks were coming sober and the screaming made them look
down at their hands, streaked with red fish blood.
The birders wanted us to find a quicker way to kill the fish —
Okay, you try, we said.

Then it drops like a curtain, the heavy velvet of dysmemory.
I guess the sandpipers wobbled in the tide pools in the rocks.
The birders withered back into the spaces in the brush.
And someone cut off the halibut's cheeks.

The reason why it's vague is: all I wanted was the drunks,
bunch of snaggletoothed losers who lived in trailers in the woods.
In those days I was drawn to the wind-chapped hand.
Good Lord, how they stank.

Question: how big does a stick have to be to be a club?
Answer: at least as big around as a small man's wrist.
Too big, and the club starts to turn into a log.
And the drunks start to stagger when they raise it for their blows.

So how far back for yore? First the story needs to skip
the part where the club has bits of brain stuck to the wood.
Instead, cut to the evening when we chopped the fish in pieces
and ate them fried in butter that left a halo around our mouths.

from Book of Bob

INVOCATION WITH LANGUAGE IMPRECISE

Now he's dead, and so I guess
I could have him say anything I want.
My father's mouth I could fill with flowers
but beauty meant less to him than plain old bread.
Let it be bread then. Let him be Bob.
Let everything go by its plainest name —
including the dirt and the bones inside it,
the secret bones inside the dirt.
Many jockeys have come to unseemly ends,
many horses were sent down to their graves
when their intricate, delicate knuckles unknitted
down a muddy track's back stretch.
But some of them rose and hobbled on,
their manes awash with blood and sweat,
the lather running from their mouths,
the ridden, the risen, the riven, the roans —
which he called *ponies*
though they weren't all that small.

CANTICLE FROM THE BOOK OF BOB

We hired the men to carry the coffin,
we hired a woman to sing in our stead.
We hired a limo, we hired a driver,
we hired each lily to stand with its head

held up and held open while scripture was read.
We hired a dustpan, we hired a broom
to sweep up the pollen that fell in the room
where we'd hired some air

to draw out the stale chord
from the organ we hired.
And we hired some tears because our own eyes were tired.

The pulpit we hired, we hired the priest
to say a few words about the deceased,

and money changed hands
and the process was brief.
We said, "Body of Christ."
Then we hired our grief.

We hired some young men to carry the coffin,
we hired a woman to sing for his soul —
we hired the limo, we hired the driver,
then we hired the ground and we hired the hole.

My Eulogy Was Deemed Too Strange

My father battled two fire-breathing white owls
that night with his sword, though he was small
and they taller than the turrets — his blade
swung only as far as their thighs.
He was dressed like an Apollo astronaut
and we were driving toward the pancake house

when we saw the castle, beset by flames.
That's when my father pulled off the road
and got embroiled in what this is: first dream
I ever dreamed. Come morning, I wanted to ask
if the fire had happened, if the others had seen
his silver boots, as delicate as carpet slippers.

But I kept my mouth shut, because — though I couldn't
distinguish the owls from the rest of the weirdness
that passes for life at the age of five — I knew
how it sounded to sound like a fool. And now
I know this: that the castle stood in the same spot
by the rise in the road to the pancake house

as where we laid him out when his time came.
Not a castle at all but a funeral home
in whose next room resided a dead fireman
whose brethren arrived in dress uniform
and paid their respects to my dad's coffin
until they realized their mistake. Outside,

the fire truck's lights swept across the wet window,
making our faces glow and dim and glow again.

But my mother looked nervous when I tried to explain
how it started in flames in the place where it ended.
As if she could see me chest-deep in the pulpit
with the book of Nostradamus and a tarot deck.

So at Mass the next day I held my tongue
and used it only as a platform for the wafer, the body of Christ,
about whom my father had his doubts. I just wish
I'd told him this while he was living: how he climbed
that bird's leg like a vine. How bravely he carried
his sword in his teeth, and how his fists were full of feathers.

Conscription Papers

Here is the trouble with visiting the past:
it means dallying so long in the company of the dead.
And they brew their tea from such strange bark—
going down, it stings.

Hence my mother sends these tea-tan sheets
gone to powder in their creases.
Official business from the War Department:
You are now a soldier in the Army of the United States! Congratulations!

The irregular print of the 1940s
clots the windows of the *e*'s and *g*'s
where the metal arms swung from the typewriter well—
Cooperate by taking only small items which can be carried in your pockets.

Like a Saint Christopher medal to deflect the bullet.
Though the dead make good duffel bags for hunkering behind,
lugging them is a son of a bitch. So my mother
is a patriot, especially when she says, *Don't put me in your poem.*

His Soldier's Pay Record tells you what kind of people we are
because nothing is declared inside its little oaktag book
but his name, rank, and serial number, forget about
posterity—even my father's signature's in pencil.

At least war gives a man an afterlife as paperwork.
Somebody named S.J. Duboff witnessed its delivery.
Odds are he's dead, so to mourn him I'll say: *Mr. Duboff,*
may your soul be of the ilk that can embrace the accident of being here.

And I know this is only a less-ochre echo of those other pages,
which I would tape here if they were not such frail
darkening scraps, about which my mother writes:
I don't want these so do with them what you will.

Night Festival, Olympia

Something about the parade I hated —
so much gaiety on a knife edge,
the captain of the samba band dressed up like a beast.
But hey, that's just me, the truculent me.
There is nothing inherently wrong with the idea
of humans being happy. As the thief says,
This will go easier if everyone cooperates.
So when a drunk stepped forward and asked for a quarter
I said, "How about a buck instead?"
with an exuberance rigged up to balance my mood:
I dug for the dollar, he stuck out his hand.
Then said, "I am a veteran," after I'd launched
my half of the shake, realizing then
the hand wasn't being offered: it was a proof.
As in: a mathematical summation.
He was showing me he had no fingers,
only two stubs whose taut raw skin
reflected pink tones with which the night glowed
as if we did not live in houses,
as if we huddled around the flames.
But this was in the parking lot at Safeway,
palace of the all-night goddess of cigs —
whose dull voltage lit my piety
when he held up his hand and I went ahead
with touching it, as if I were not afraid.

Eulogy from the Boardwalk behind the KFC

Deschutes Parkway, 10/11/01

What is not part of the calamity goes on —
the salmon move upstream. Their colors
are borrowed from the heart of the water,
a camouflage blotchwork
of old bruises. They zigzag forth
in single file — tack left, tack right,
then pause and shiver, tack and shiver,
tack and shiver, tack and shatter —
when their shivering scatters
and leaves nothing at the core.
They get their discipline from the current
and go crazy in the calm — please notify
the human spectators: what is not part
goes crazy in the calm. The fish
are slightly darker than the water
whose feet we lay our shadows at —
all right, I know the water doesn't have feet
but how much precision do you expect
from us who stand here all strung out
on far-flung grief? At least I have tried
to describe the salmon honestly,
their knitted frenzy below the floodgate.
How we see them only if we look straight down
from this low bridge, where the cars scream past.
Straight down, and the water surface unsilvers:
what we see best are their white scars.

Shrike Tree

Most days back then I would walk by the shrike tree,
a dead hawthorn at the base of a hill.
The shrike had pinned smaller birds on the tree's black thorns
and the sun had stripped them of their feathers.

Some of the dead ones hung at eye level
while some burned holes in the sky overhead.
At least it is honest,
the body apparent
and not rotting in the dirt.

And I, having never seen the shrike at work,
can only imagine how the breasts were driven into the branches.
When I saw him he'd be watching from a different tree
with his mask like Zorro
and the gray cape of his wings.

At first glance he could have been a mockingbird or a jay
if you didn't take note of how his beak was hooked.
If you didn't know the ruthlessness of what he did —
ah, but that is a human judgment.

They are mute, of course, a silence at the center of a bigger silence,
these rawhide ornaments, their bald skulls showing.
And notice how I've slipped into the present tense
as if they were still with me.

Of course they are still with me.

They hang there, desiccating
by the trail where I walked, back when I could walk,
before life pinned me on its thorn.
It is ferocious, life, but it must eat,
then leaves us with the artifact.

Which is: these black silhouettes in the midday sun,
strict and jagged, like an Asian script.
A tragedy that is not without its glamour.
Not without the runes of the wizened meat.

Because imagine the luck! — to be plucked from the air,
to be drenched and dried in the sun's bright voltage —
well, hard luck is luck, nonetheless.
With a chunk of sky in each eye socket.
And the pierced heart strung up like a pearl.

Chum

How come we all don't have the luxury of our ghosts?
The way some paintings of salmon
show their spectral versions flying.
License, you might say,
for the artist to put dead fish in the sky.
Instead of leaving them as they are
when you see them wilting in the eddy:
two tons of major spent-sex stink.

Yet see how everyone skips so giddily around the trail —
eyeballing the spawning from this cedar bridge.
As if they're sure we will be cohorts
in the rapture about which the bumper stickers speak,
as if we really will ascend someday to swim among the fishes.
All of us: see how good we are,
so careful not to kick stones down into the creek.

I'm just trying to get a handle on how it would be
if we made love one time in our lives
(after days spent on the interstate)
before we lay down to die so publicly in shallow pools?
While the other forms pass by and point
to educate their frenzied children:
See the odd species. They chose love.

from

Inseminating the Elephant

(2009)

Any idiot can face a crisis; it is this day-to-day living that wears
you out.

CHEKHOV

Virtue Is the Best Helmet

One of these days I'm going to get myself an avatar
so I can ride an archaeopteryx in cyberspace —
goodbye, the meat cage.
Pray the server doesn't crash, pray
against the curse of carpal tunnel syndrome.

But then my friend the lactation consultant
brings up the quadriplegic who gave birth
(two times no less)
(motorcycle wreck)
just to make her body do
one thing the meat could still remember.

Somebody has to position the babies
to sip the breastmilk rivulets.
And the cells exude
despite their slumber. One minute
too much silence, the next there's so much screaming.

Turns out Madagascar's giant cockroach
makes a good addition to a robot
because the living brain adds up to more than: motor,
tracking ball, and the binary numeric code.

Usually the cockroach flees from light,
but sometimes it stands in its little coach unmoving,
stymied by the dumb fact of air.

And sometimes it rams into a wall
to force reality to show its hand.

Found Object

Somebody left this white T-shirt
like a hangman's hood on the new parking meter —
the magic marks upon its back say: *I QUIT METH 4-EVER.*
A declaration to the sky, whose angels all wear seagull wings
swooping over this street with its torn scratch tickets
and Big Gulp cups dropped by the curb.

Extra large, it has been customized
with a pocketknife or a canine tooth
to rough the armholes where my boobs now wobble
as I roam these rooms lit by twilight's bulb,
feeling half like Bette Davis in a wheelchair
and half like that Hell's Angels kingpin with the tracheotomy.

Dear reader, do you know that guy?
I didn't think so. If only we could all watch the same TV.
But no doubt you have seen the gulls flying,
and also the sinister bulked-up crows
carrying white clouds of hotdog buns in their beaks:
you can promise them you'll straighten up, but they are such big cynics.

I should have told you *My lotto #'s 2-11-19-23-36*
is what's written in front, beside the silk screen
for Listerine Cool Mint PocketPaks™ —
which means you can't hijack my name;
no, you have to go find your own, like a Hopi brave.
You might have to sit in a sweat lodge until you pass out

or eat a weird vine and it will not be pleasant. Your pulse
goes staccato like a Teletype machine — then *blam*

you'll be transformed into your post-larval being.
Maybe swallowtail, maybe moth: trust me, I know
because once I was a baby-blue convertible
but now I'm this black hot rod painted with flames.

Rebuttal

My quarrel with the Old Masters is: they never made suffering big enough—
that tiny leg sliding into the bay almost *insults* me,
that it should be all we get of the falling boy after the half-hour stunt
of his famous flying. *Don't you see*
they are cartoons? the drunk hissed
in the British Museum, a drunk in a sport coat
that made him look credible at first, some kind of docent,
an itinerant purveyor of glosses that left me
confused. I studied Brueghel's paintings, tiny
skaters, and hunters come home with tiny dead animals
gutted outside the frame, where the tiny offal
presumably had been left. I was looking for *Icarus*
but the *Musée des Beaux-Arts is in Belgium you twit*
and so I did not see the plowman wearing his inexplicably
dainty shoes, *a cartoon you American sow,*
and no one came to my rescue in that gallery vacated
even by its dust. Where I also did not see the galleon
anchored below the plowman's pasture with its oblivious,
content-with-being-tiny sheep. But just wait

until that ship sails out
and encounters the kind of storm that'll require Abstract
Expressionism to capture the full feeling of.
The giant canvases of the twentieth century!
Swaths of color with no figures in them at all!
How immense the drowning when you're the boy who drowns.
Between the fireball on your back and the water in front
all gray and everywhere and hard as concrete when you smack down.

A Romance

As a child, I saw a child set down her binder like a wall
through the candy bin at the Corner Luncheonette
so she could shoplift gum while she spoke to the clerk —

and from that moment was in love: *Oh theft.*

College was supposed to straighten me
like a bent tree strangled by a wire,
but being done with sweetness I could not resist the lure of meat.

How the red muscle gleamed in its shiny wrap,
a wedge that had once been the thigh or the loin
of a slow brute's body, sugar-dirt and clotted grass

to be snatched in an instant
and zipped into the crone-y-est of pocketbooks.
Radiance housed in rawhide again, as when it was living.

A steak can be stuck in your jeans when you're skinny,
a rump roast is right for a puffy down coat,
small chops will fit under a thin peasant blouse

where it falls off the breasts
like a woodland river
with a limestone amphitheater underneath.

Ancient city, ancient sublet, ancient wooden fire escape —
with my other bandits I learned to say how-de-do in French.
We were yanking on the cord that would start the motor of our lives

though we did not have the choke adjusted yet.

Sometimes it seemed I floated in the dregs like a tea bag
bloating up with facts.
Until a girl ran in the door, panting hard, face red,

slab thudding
from her snowflake-damasked waist onto the table,
and we stood around it gawking at the way it seemed to breathe.

from Notes from My Apprenticeship

THE CHAMBER

As does the poem by William Blake, this involves a poison worm,
        a worm that would make the blackbird who ate it
            flap and squawk in distress

while at regular intervals I played a tape of a bird
        also squawking in distress, so you see
            there was this salt-box-girl regression going on

while I took notes: *Now the bird is squawking in distress,*
        my job being to watch on closed-circuit TV
            and record the bird's death, were that to occur

in the chamber made from a gutted fridge
        rigged up to a button in the next room
            where, when I pushed, I'd hear a musical *plink*

over the loudspeaker as a mealworm dropped
        from a crown of vials that sat on the chamber,
            the crown rotating as the glass vials tipped,

one worm per plink, though I sometimes plinked twice
        if the worm got stuck
            or if the bird failed to squawk

in that tiny brick building that rustled with wings
        from birds scritching in cages
            I'd been filling for weeks,

my truck full of traps I set on fence posts at dawn,
       when the redwings clung
              to tall blades in the ditches

and sang *shuck-shreeek* as the dirt road fumed
       behind me in the mirrors, unveiling a rising
              red-winged sun that I drove into

feeling immortal,
       how could I not feel immortal
              when I was mistress of the poison worm?

SUPER 8

There were so many black birds I could not count,
homing on this patch of dusk. My boss's idea
had been to spray them with spangles
so that, if found, the finder would know
the bird had stopped here at this cornfield
behind the Super 8 motel. That is,
if he could imagine the helicopter
with its tank of glue and light.
Otherwise, he might just wonder at a spangled bird.

We untangled them from the mist nets
and brought them into the bathroom's white tile grid
thirty feet east of the blacktop stripe,
where I counted the spangles, a soldier
in the tribe of useless data. Afterward
I walked them back outside two at a time
and opened my fists, where the birds paused
just long enough to leave their own data on my palms.
Here's what we think of
your spangles, your starlight. Then the night flushed
them up into its swoon — however faintly,
the corn glittered as the birds resumed their ravening.

Incubus

While the spectacular round butt of the fat junkie sitting on the curb
rotated upward from his belt —

the legs of the skinny junkie wriggled upward from a dumpster.
And when he stood, I saw
his familiar figure, thinned —

two times he'd snipped my kitchen with the scissors of his hips
while he directed stories from the rehab clinic toward us
ladies in our panty hose,

our fingers sliding up and down our wineglass stems.

Later, in the cloak of his jean jacket,
he slipped upstairs and stole my pharmaceuticals,
my legitimate pharmaceuticals! —

so an awkwardness descended on the realm of gestures
there in the alley behind the YMCA, where I looked at any alternate —
pothole, hydrant, not buttocks,
don't look at buttocks, don't look at dumpster, don't. Look:

I would have been a crone to him,
and he would have been my pirate son,
my son who sleeps beneath the bridge

in the cloak of his jean jacket, dabbed with fecal matter now.

Still, when he comes at night,
brass button by button
and blade by blade — his skinny thighs —

I open myself like a medicine cabinet
and let him take the pill bottles from my breasts.

First Epistle of Lucia to Her Old Boyfriends

Not infrequently I find myself wondering which of you are dead
now that it's been so long since I have had a boyfriend
for whom this wonder would be a somewhat milder version of
the way our actual parting went — i.e., with me not wondering
but outright wishing that an outright lightning bolt
would sail sharply into your thick heads.

Can I plead youth now over malign intent?
And does my moral fiber matter anyhow
since I have not gone forth and et cetera'd —
i.e., doesn't my absent children's nondepletion of the ozone layer
give me some atmospheric exchange credits under the Kyoto Protocol
to release the fluorocarbons of these unkind thoughts?

Anyhow what is the likelihood of you old boyfriends reading this
even if you are not dead? Be assured your end is hypothetical.
Also be assured I blush most furiously
whenever that tower room in Ensenada comes to mind
where the mescal functioned as an exchange credit for those lies you told
about your Alford pleas and your ex-wives who turned out not ex at all.

Anyhow the acid rain has caused my lightning to go limp
over bungalows where you have partial custody of your teenagers
and AA affirmations magneted to the fridge
from which your near beers sweat as you wonder if I'm dead,
since the exchange for this-here wonder is your wonder about me.
Even though it shows my nerve — to think you'd think of me at all —

I await word of your undeadness

PS: along with your mild version of my just reward.

Raised Not by Wolves

The family sank into its sorrows —
we softened like noodles in a pot.
Whereas the bicycle's bones were painted gold
and stood firm against the house
no matter how hard it rained.

Beneath the handlebar mount, it said ROYAL in red letters
unscathed despite the elements;
this was the bicycle's first lesson,
to be royal and unscathed —

I pressed my ear-cup to the welds.

Pedal furiously, then coast in silence.
You will need teeth to grab the chain.
Exhortations with the stringent priggishness of Zen,
delivered by a guru who hauls you off and wallops you

in answer to your simple question.

Though its demise is foggy,
I can conjure with precision its rebukes, the dull sting
when the boy-bar bashed my private place.

Then no talking was permitted
beyond one stifled yelp.

You could, however, rub the wound
with the meat of your thumb — so long
as you did this stealthily, pretending you had an itch.

Job Site, 1967

Brick laid down, scritch of the trowel's
downward stroke, another brick set
then the flat side of the trowel moving
across the top of the course of bricks.
My father stepped from the car in his brown loafers,
the rest of him is fading but not his loafers,
the round spot distended by his big toe.
Brick laid down, scritch of the trowel's
downward stroke, the silver bulb of the door lock
sticking up as I sat in the car,
the kid in the dress. Newark burned
just over the river, not so far south
as the South of their skin — deepening
under the ointment of sweat, skin and sweat
they'd hauled from the South
brother by brother and cousin by cousin
to build brick walls for men like my father
while Newark burned, and Plainfield burned,
while the men kept their rhythm, another brick set,
then the flat side of the trowel moving
across the top as my father crossed the mud.
I sat in the car with the silver bulb of the door lock
sticking up, though I was afraid,
the kid in the dress, the trowel moving
across the top of the course of bricks.
You can't burn a brick,
you smashed a brick through a window,
the downward stroke, another brick set,
but to get the window first you needed a wall,
and they were building the wall,

they were building the wall
while my father, in his brown loafers,
stepped toward them with their pay.

Postcard from Florida

After paddling out, I found the manatees
in canals behind the pricey homes,
as I once found the endangered Hawaiian goose

beside the hulks that once were dream cars.
So the scarce beast gets its camouflage
at the farthest outpost of our expectations:

the gators prefer golf courses to marshes,
prefer Cheetos, Fritos, nachos, Ho Hos
to baby fish as bright as coins.

What doesn't kill us makes us strong
(see the scar where propellers have cut through the hide),
but doesn't that mean some of us *will* be killed

and not made strong? My sweet flabbies
swing their gum-rubber hips in freshwater
murmuring from the air-conditioning compressors

and waggle my little boat with their bristles —
what doesn't capsize us
makes us give a whopper sigh.

Look up, and a geezer by his pool
feeds a great blue heron from his hand:
they are so alike they could be twins, him croaking

a tune the bird has come to know
and stalks at certain times of day.
Meanwhile two girls next door in bathing suits

who have turned on the hose in their backyard
hop now at the edge of their wooden bulkhead
singing *Come to us humanities*

and oh see how they do.

Transcendentalism

The professor stabbed his chest with his hands curled like forks
before coughing up the question
that had dogged him since he first read Emerson:
Why am I "I"? We hunkered like musk oxen
while his lecture drifted against us like snow.
If we could, we would have turned our backs into the wind.

I felt bad about his class's being such a snoozefest, though peaceful too,
a quiet little interlude from everyone outside
rooting up the corpse of literature
for being too Caucasian. There was a simple answer
to my own question (how come no one loved me,
stomping on the pedals of my little bicycle):

I was insufferable. So, too, was Emerson I bet,
though I liked *If the red slayer think he slays* —
the professor drew a giant eyeball to depict the Over-soul.
Then he read a chapter from his own book:
naptime.
He didn't care when our heads tipped forward on their stalks.

When spring came, he even threw us a picnic in his yard
where dogwood bloomed despite a few last
dirty bergs of snow. He was a wounded animal
being chased across the tundra by those wolves,
the postmodernists. At any moment
you expected to see blood come dripping through his clothes.

And I am I who never understood his question,
though he let me climb to take a seat

aboard the wooden scow he'd been building in the shade
of thirty-odd years. How I ever rowed it
from his yard, into my life — remains a mystery.
The work is hard because the eyeball's heavy, riding in the bow.

January/Macy's/ *The Bra Event*

Word of it comes whispered by a slippery thin section
of the paper, where the models pantomime unruffled tête-à-têtes
despite the absence of their blouses.

Each year when my familiar latches on them so intently
like a grand master plotting the white queen's path,
like a baby trying to suckle a whole roast beef,

I ask: What, you salt block, are you dreaming
about being clubbed by thunderheads? — but he will not say.
Meanwhile Capricorn's dark hours flabbed me,

uneasy about surrendering to the *expert fitter*
(even if the cupped hands were licensed and bonded) —
I had August in mind, seeing the pygmy goats at the county fair.

Now the sky is having its daily rain event
and the trees are having their hibernal bark event,
pretending they feel unruffled

despite the absence of their leaves. And we forget how they looked
all flouncy and green. Instead we regard
fearfully the sway of their old trunks.

The Van with the Plane

At first I didn't get it: I thought it was just scrap metal roped on the roof
of this dented ancient Econoline van
with its parrot-yellow burden.
Bright mishmash so precarious
my heart twitched whenever I had to tail it down the road
until one day I woke to it: you blockhead, that's a *plane*.

I don't know how I missed it — of course it was a plane,
disassembled, with one yellow wing pointing sideways from the roof.
Fuselage dinged by rocks from the road
and two little wheels sticking up from the van —
now when I tally all the pieces, it seems pretty obvious.
And I wonder if toting it around would be a burden

or more some kind of anti-burden.
Because if you drove around with a plane
you might feel less fettered than the rest of us:
say your life hung around your neck like a concrete Elizabethan ruff
you could always ditch that junker van
and take off rattling down the runway of the road.

But my friends said they'd seen that clunker so long on the road
it was like a knock-knock joke heard twice too often.
You'll be sorry they said when I went looking for the guy who drove the van,
whom I found in the library, beating the dead horse of his plane.
Once you got him started it was hard to shut him off:
how, if he had field to rise from, he'd fly to Sitka, or Corvallis—

but how does a guy living in a van get a field, you think the IRS
just goes around giving people fields for free? The road

of his thought was labyrinthine and sometimes ended in the rough
of Cambodia or Richard Nixon.
He said a plane in pieces still counts as a plane,
it was still a good plane, it was just a plane on a van.

And of course I liked him better as part and parcel of the van;
the actual guy could drive you nuts.
All his grace depended on his sitting underneath that plane
as it rattles up and down the road
like a train with a missile, a warhead of heavy hydrogen.
Because the van reverts to rubble once the plane takes off.

And if my own life is a plane, it's like the *Spirit of St. Louis* —
no windshield, just the vantage of a periscope.
Forward, onward, never look down — at the burden of these roofs and roads.

Snowstorm with Inmates and Dogs

The prison kennel's tin roof howls
while the dogs romp outside through the flakes.
The inmates trained a dog to lift my legs —
for months they rolled the concrete floor
in wheelchairs, simulating.

Through a window I watch them cartwheel now,
gray sweatpants rising against the whitened hill
traversed by wire asterisks and coils.
At first I feared they pitied me,
the way I flinched at the building's smell.

Now the tin roof howls, the lights go off
to the sound of locking doors. Go on, breathe —
no way the machinery of my lungs
is going to plow the county road.
Didn't I try to run over a guy,

spurned love being the kindling stick that rubbed
against his IOUs? Easy to land here,
anyone could — though I think laughter
would elude me, no matter what the weather.
Compared to calculating how far to the road.

Signs there say: CORRECTIONS CENTER DO NOT PICK UP HITCHHIKERS.
My instructions were: Accept no notes or photographs,
and restrict the conversation to such topics as
how to teach the dog to nudge
the light switch with his nose.

Now the women let their snowballs fly — as if
the past were a simple matter that could splat and melt.
Only my red dog turns his head
toward the pines beyond the final fence
before the generator chugs to life.

Early Cascade

I couldn't have waited. By the time you return
it would have rotted on the vine.
So I cut the first tomato into eighths,
salted the pieces in the dusk,
and found the flesh not mealy (like last year)
or bitter,
even when I swallowed the green crown of the stem
that made my throat feel dusty and warm.

Pah. I could have gagged on the sweetness.
The miser accused by her red sums.
Better had I eaten the dirt itself
on this the first night in my life
when I have not been too busy for my loneliness —
at last, it comes.

Twenty-Five Thousand Volts per Inch

The weird summer of lightning (to be honest) was not a summer, but a week
when we sat every night in a far corner of the yard
to watch the silver twitch over our drinks.
It may help to know the sky hardly ever spasms here,
which is why we savored the postscript smell of nickel,
ions crisping in the deep fry.

The bolts made everything erogenous, the poppies and the pumpkin vine —
we could hardly bear to leave our watch post
but had tickets for the concert at the pier.
And we could not bear to miss the jam band from our youth,
which we feared discovering lacked talent and looked foolish
in their caveman belt buckles and leather hats.

Whew. That we found in them a soulfulness, an architecture
of tempo changes and chord progressions
left us relieved. Childishly
we hummed along as the sun got gulped down like a vitamin
and boats of cheapskates gathered on the bay.
When the lightning started, it was fearsome and silent

as usual. We were older, we knew this,
but the past proved not to be all suicide and motorcycle accidents.
Here was proof the music had shown some finesse —
even if it pillaged the discographies of black men from the Delta
it did so honorably, *erotically*, meaning
"that which gathers." So we held hands and drew near.

And the flashes lit us, when they lit us, in platinum flames:
then we saw, behold, below the bleachers,

a man whose rubber sneaker toe-tips
punctured the darkness as he spun.
He lurched and spun and lurched and fell,
a messenger from the ancient cults

until his stomach's contents were strobed ruthlessly
once they splattered on the tarmac. Sky says: *Rise,*
feet say: *Heavy.* Body would say: *Torn in two*
if it weren't already passed out
with all the good Samaritans busy remembering
the words to the tune about the rambling man. Oh

Bacchus, Dionysus, ye Southern rock stars
of antiquity: Thank you for shutting the black door
behind which he vanished, so we could resume
holding each other, like two swigs of mouthwash.
Then the brother who was not dead
played another of our childhood songs.

The Garbo Cloth

Her daughter wrote back to say my friend had died
      (my friend to whom I wrote a letter maybe twice a year).
From time to time I'd pictured her amid strange foliage
      (and in a Mongol yurt, for she was fond of travel).
Why not a flock of something darkening the sky, so we would know
      (*ah, so-and-so is gone!*)?
For a woman from the city, this might perhaps be pigeons
      (blacking out the sun).
Or else a human messenger, as once when she was fabric-shopping
      (bolt of green silk furled across her body)
Garbo passed, and nodded. At Macy's years ago
      (when I was not a creature in her world).
Of course she bought the cloth, but never sewed the dress
      ("a massive stroke, and I take comfort in the fact she felt no pain").
Logic says we should make omens of our Garbos and our birds
      (but which one bears the message? which one just the mess?).
From the kayak, I've seen pigeons nesting underneath the pier
      (a dim ammoniated stink)
where one flew into my face. I read this as a sign
      (that rancid smash of feathers)
but couldn't fathom what it meant, the bird trapped in the lag time
      (of an oracle's translation).
Foolish mind, wanting to obliterate the lag and why —
      (let memory wait to catch up to its sorrow).

A Pedantry

Many of the great men — Buddha, Saint Augustine,
Jefferson, Einstein — had a woman and child
they needed to ditch. A little prologue
before the great accomplishments could happen.

From nothing came this bloody turnip
umbilicaled to the once-beloved,
only now she's transformed like a Hindu god
with an animal snout and too many limbs.

You'd rather board a steamer with chalk dust on your pants
or sit under a bo tree and be pelted by flaming rocks,
renounce the flesh
or ride off on a stallion —

there is no papoose designed for such purposes,
plus the baby would have to be sedated.
Sorry.
We don't want the future to fall into the hands of the wrong -ists!

That's how civilization came into being
for us who remained in the doorways of here,
our companions those kids who became chimney sweeps, car thieves,
and makers of lace.

By day we live in the shadows of theories; by night
the moon holds us in its regard
when it doesn't have more important business
on the back side of the clouds.

Martha

> Nearly all the remaining quarter million passenger pigeons were
> killed in one day in 1896.

They named the last one Martha,
and she died September 1st, 1914, in the Cincinnati Zoo,
she who was once one of so many billions
the sky went dark for days
when they flew past.
Makes me wonder what else could go,

some multitudinous widget like clouds or leaves
or the jellyfish ghosting the water in autumn
or the shore-shards of crushed clams?
Goodbye kisses:
once I had so many of you but now I note
your numbers growing slim —

yesterday a man stood me up in the sea
behind the big rock where the sand dollars live.
And when I said *Now we should kiss*
it seemed we'd grown too peculiar
and I thought: Oh-ho kisses, are you leaving too
like the man's hair? Or like

the taut bellies we once had
or the menstrual period that was mine alone —
time flew its coop
our days did skid
and now see my commas going too —
art mimicking life's mortal nature?

So I did no hem-haw with the man
I told him to grab hold of my ears
since daylight burned
the tide had begun to apply its suction then
the shotguns of our lips turned toward
what was perhaps the last of our wild flock.

Breaking News

They found the missing bride and she is living.
They found the boys floating on the ocean in their little yellow raft.
The ornithologists found the extinct woodpecker
when it flew over their canoe.
Not everyone is convinced, though.
One recording of its distinctive knock turned out to be a gunshot.

A century of Ozark fishermen
said they saw the bird when they were stranded
on their hummocks in the swamp.
Nobody believed them but the catfish in their pails.
Those boys thought their muscles strong enough to paddle against the squall.
And the bride only wanted a bus trip west
before the rest of her life downed her like an olive.

Sometimes survival strikes us dumb
with the improbable story of resurrection;
we see the blossoms smutted on the ground
turning back into a flowering tree. Next year
there'll be new nettle stalks
to sting your fingers, which you'll drag
through the serrated leaves to prove
the world has not lost the consolation of its old pain.

For the First Crow with West Nile Virus to Arrive in Our State

For a long time you lay tipped on your side like a bicycle
but now your pedaling has stopped. Already
the mosquitoes have chugged their blisterful of blood
and flown on. Time moves forward,
no cause to weep, I keep reminding myself of this:
the body will accrue its symptoms. And the handbooks,
which warn us not to use the absolutes, are wrong:
the body will *always* accrue its symptoms.

But shouldn't there also be some hatchlings within view:
sufficient birth to countervail the death?
At least a zero on the bottom line:
I'm not asking for black integers,
just for nature not to drive our balance into the dirt.

What should we utter over the broken glass that marks your grave?
The bird books give us mating calls but not too many death songs.
And whereas the Jews have their Kaddish and the Tibetans
have their strident prayers, all I'm impelled to do is sweet-talk
the barricades of heaven. Where you my vector
soar already, a sore thumb among the clouds.

Still I can see in the denuded maple one of last year's nests
waiting to be filled again, a ragged mass of sticks.
Soon the splintered shells will fill it
as your new geeks claim the sky — any burgling
of bloodstreams starts when something yolky breaks.
And I write this as if language could give restitution for the breakage
or make you lift your head from its quilt of wayside trash.
Or retract the mosquito's proboscis, but that's language again,
whose five-dollar words not even can unmake you.

Altered Beast

You were a man and I used to be a woman
before we first put our quarters in

the game at the gas station, whose snack-chip display
wore a film of oil and soot

beside which you turned into a green gargoyle and then
a flying purple lynx —

whereas I could not get the hang of the joystick
and remained as I began

while you kicked my jaw and chopped my spine,
a beating I loved because it meant you were rising

fast through the levels — and the weak glom on
via defeat, which is better than nothing —

insert sound effects here: *blip blat ching ching,*

and when they stopped, your claws gripped the naked
-looking pink lizard that I was,

blood-striped and ragged, as if being a trophy
were the one reward the vanquished get —

which is why, walking home through the curbside sludge,
when you held my hand with your arm outstretched

as if you were holding a dripping scalp or head,
I hummed with joy to be your spoils.

On the Chehalis River

All day long the sun is busy, going up and going down,
and the moon is busy, swinging the lasso of its gravity.
And the clouds are busy, metamorphing as they skid —
the vultures are busy, circling in their kettle.

And the river is busy filling up my britches
as I sit meditating in the shallows until my legs go numb.
Upstream I saw salmon arching half into the air:
glossy slabs of muscle I first thought were seals.

They roiled in a deeper pocket of the river,
snagged in a drift net on Indian land.
Trying to leap free before relenting to the net
with a whack of final protest from the battered tail.

They'll be clubbed, I know, when the net's hauled up
but if there were no net they'd die anyway when they breed.
You wonder how it *feels* to them: their ardent drive upstream.
What message is delivered when the eggs release.

A heron sums a theory with one crude croak; the swallows
write page after page of cursive in the air. My own offering
is woozy because when their bodies breached the surface
the sun lit them with a flash that left me blind.

Inseminating the Elephant

The zoologists who came from Germany
wore bicycle helmets and protective rubber suits.
So as not to be soiled by substances
that alchemize to produce laughter in the human species,
how does that work biochemically is a question
whose answer I have not found yet. But these are men
whose language requires difficult conjugations under any circumstance:
first, there's the matter of the enema, which ought to come
as no surprise. Because what the news brings us
is often wheelbarrows of dung — suffering,
with photographs. And so long as there is suffering,
there should be also baby elephants — especially this messy,
headlamp-lit calling-forth. The problem lies
in deciding which side to side with: it is natural
to choose the giant rectal thermometer
over the twisted human form,
but is there something cowardly in that comic swerve?
Hurry an elephant
to carry the bundle of my pains,
another with shiny clamps and calipers
and the anodyne of laughter. So there, now I've alluded
to my body that grows ever more inert — better not overdo
lest you get scared, the sorrowing world
is way too big. How the zoologists start
is by facing the mirror of her flanks,
that foreboding luscious place where the gray hide
gives way to a zeroing-in of skin as vulnerable as an orchid.
Which is the place to enter, provided you are brave,
brave enough to insert your laser-guided camera
to avoid the two false openings of her "vestibule,"

much like the way of entering death, of giving birth to death,
calling it forth as described in the Tibetan Book.
And are you brave enough to side with laughter
if I face my purplish, raw reflection
and attempt the difficult entry of that chamber where
the seed-pearl of my farce and equally opalescent sorrow
lie waiting?

For the Mad Cow in Tenino

I don't know where you rank in my list of killers:
my viral load, my sociopaths, my inattention
on the interstate, where I crane my head after the hawk
and the windshield splatters
into diamonds. Not just thinking about the hawk,
or even merely watching it, I always have to *be* it for a minute,
just as my mind enters the murderers
for one long flash before it stumbles out.

From your postmortem, you held us fast
while a man said *It's enough* as his lungs filled
after being stabbed here near the playground,
before they milled his limbs with power tools
and scattered him beyond retrieval. Too late
to recall your brain, and the fatty white part of your spine,
already delivered to the rendering plant
and melted down into the slurry.

That night is gone and cannot be reassembled
despite my re-imagining the car
with a man dying in its trunk, a car otherwise like any other,
as we could not verify your affliction
for days after you fell. Which left the land in chaos
except for Scatter Creek's flowing past,
wending without hurry through the coastal range
before it empties rain and blood into Willapa Bay.

from

On the Spectrum of Possible Deaths

(2012)

No death for you. You are involved.
WELDON KEES

The Second Slaughter

Achilles slays the man who slew his friend, pierces the corpse
behind the heels and drags it
behind his chariot like the cans that trail
a bride and groom. Then he lays out
a banquet for his men, oxen and goats
and pigs and sheep; the soldiers eat
until a greasy moonbeam lights their beards.

The first slaughter is for victory, but the second slaughter is for grief—
in the morning more animals must be killed
for burning with the body of the friend. But Achilles finds
no consolation in the hiss and crackle of their fat;
not even heaving four stallions on the pyre
can lift the ballast of his sorrow.

And here I turn my back on the epic hero—the one who slits
the throats of his friend's dogs,
killing what the loved one loved
to reverse the polarity of grief. Let him repent
by vanishing from my concern
after he throws the dogs onto the fire.
The singed fur makes the air too difficult to breathe.

When the oil wells of Persia burned I did not weep
until I heard about the birds, the long-legged ones especially
which I imagined to be scarlet, with crests like egrets
and tails like peacocks, covered in tar
weighting the feathers they dragged through black shallows
at the rim of the marsh. But once

I told this to a man who said I was inhuman, for giving animals
my first lament. So now I guard
my inhumanity like the jackal
who appears behind the army base at dusk,
come there for scraps with his head lowered
in a posture that looks like appeasement
though it is not.

Again, the Body

> I have become what I have always been and it has taken a lifetime, all of my own life, to reach this point where it is as if I know finally that I am alive and that I am here, right now.
>
> TOBIAS SCHNEEBAUM, *KEEP THE RIVER ON YOUR RIGHT*

When you spend many hours alone in a room
you have more than the usual chances to disgust yourself—
this is the problem of the body, not that it is mortal
but that it is mortifying. When we were young they taught us
do not touch it, but who can keep from touching it,
from scratching off the juicy scab? Today I bit
a thick hangnail and thought of Schneebaum,
who walked four days into the jungle
and stayed for the kindness of the tribe—
who would have thought that cannibals would be so tender?
This could be any life: the vegetation is thick
and when there is an opening, you follow
down its tunnel until one night you find yourself
walking as on any night, though of a sudden your beloved
friends are using their stone blades
to split the skulls of other men. Gore everywhere,
though the chunk I ate was bland;
it was only when I chewed too far and bled
that the taste turned satisfyingly salty.
How difficult to be in a body,
how easy to be repelled by it,
eating one-sixth of the human heart.
Afterward, the hunters rested
their heads on one another's thighs
while the moon shone on the river
for the time it took to cross the narrow sky
making its gash through the trees...

To the Field of Scotch Broom That Will Be Buried by the New Wing of the Mall

Half costume jewel, half parasite, you stood
swaying to the music of cash registers in the distance
while a helicopter chewed the linings
of the clouds above the clear-cuts.
And I forgave the pollen count
while cabbage moths teased up my hair
before your flowers fell apart when they
turned into seeds. How resigned you were
to your oblivion, unlistening to the cumuli
as they swept past. And soon those gusts
will mill you, when the backhoe comes
to dredge your roots, but that is not
what most impends, as the chopper descends
to the hospital roof so that somebody's heart
can be massaged back into its old habits.

Mine went a little haywire
at the crest of the road, on whose other side
you lay in blossom.
As if your purpose were to defibrillate me
with a thousand electrodes,
one volt each.

Domestic

Here the coyote lives in shadows between houses,
feeds by running west to raid the trash behind the store
where they sell food that comes in cans
yesterday expired. Picture it
perching on the dumpster, a corrugated
sheet of metal welded to the straight, its haunch
accruing the imprint of the edge until it pounces,
skittering on the cans. It has tried
to gnaw them open and broken all its teeth.

Bald-flanked, rheumy-eyed, sniffing the wheels
of our big plastic trash carts but too pigeon-
chested to knock them down, scat full of eggshells
from the compost pile. "I am like that, starved,
with dreams of rutting in a culvert's narrow light — "
we mumble our affinities as we vacate into sleep.
Because we occupy the wrong animal — don't you too feel it?
Haven't you stood in the driveway, utterly confused?
Maybe you were taking out the garbage, twisting
your robe into a noose-knot at your throat, when you stopped
fighting the urge to howl, and howled —
and did it bring relief, my friend, however self-deceiving?

I Could Name Some Names

of those who have drifted through thus far of their allotted
fifty or seventy or ninety years on Earth
with no disasters happening,
whatever had to be given up was given up —
the food at the rehab facility was better than you would expect
and the children turned out more or less okay;
sure there were some shaky years
but no one's living in the basement anymore
with a divot in his head, that's where the shrapnel landed/or
don't look at her stump. It is easy
to feel possessed of a soul that's better schooled
than the fluffy cloud inside people who have never known suchlike
events by which our darlings
are unfavorably remade. And the self
is the darling's darling
($I = darling^2$). Every day
I meditate against my envy
aimed at those who drift inside the bubble of no-trouble,
— what is the percentage? 20% of us? 8%? zero?
Maybe the ex-president with his nubile daughters,
vigorous old parents, and clean colonoscopy. Grrrr.
Remember to breathe. *Breathe in suffering,*
breathe out blessings say the ancient dharma texts.
Still I beg to file this one complaint
that some are mountain-biking through the scrublands
while she is here at Ralph's Thriftway,
running her thumb over a peach's bruise,
her leg a steel rod
in a miniskirt, to make sure I see.

Cold Snap, November

The salmon corpses clog the creek without sufficient room to spin:
see, even the fish want to kill themselves this time of year
the therapist jokes. Her remedy
is to record three gratitudes a day —
so let the fish count for one, make two the glaucous gulls
who pluck the eyes before they fill
with the cloudy juice of vanishing.

But don't these monuments to *there*-ness
feel a little ostentatious? Not just the gratitudes,
but also what they used to call a hardware store
where you hike for hours underneath the ether
between the ceiling and the dropped-down lighting tubes,
muttering *I need a lock-washer for my lawnmower shroud* —
huh? You know
you should feel like Walt Whitman, celebrating
everything, but instead you feel like Pope Julius II
commanding Michelangelo to carve forty statues for his tomb.

When even one giant marble Moses feels like a bit too much.

This year made it almost to December without a frost to deflate the dahlias
and though I stared for hours at the psychedelia of their petals,

trying to coax them to apply their shock-paddles to my heart,
it wasn't working. Until one morning when
I found them black and staggering in their pails,
charred marionettes, twist-tied to their stakes, I apologize
for being less turned-on by the thing than by its going.
Not the sunset
but afterward when we stand dusted with the sunset's silt,

and not the surgical theater, even with its handsome anesthesiologist
in blue dustcap and booties — no,

his *after*'s what I'm buzzed by, the black slide into nothing
(well, someone ought to speak for it).

Or it can come in white — not so much the swirling snow
as the fallen stuff that makes the mind continuous
with the meadow that it sees.

Auntie Roach

Courage is no good:
It means not scaring others.

PHILIP LARKIN

One day George Washington rides around Mount Vernon
for five hours on his horse, the next
he's making his auspicious exodus
on the spectrum of possible deaths.
Rasputin was fed cyanide in little cakes
but did not slough his living husk,
and so Prince Felix sang to him, then mesmerized him
with a gaudy cross. And though he dropped when he was shot
he popped back up and ran outside: it was
Purishkevich who fired three times in the courtyard —
but even with his body bound
in the frozen Neva, one arm worked

its way free. Now, he must have howled
while his giblets leaked, though the cold
is reputed to be kind. Sliding his end
toward a numeral less horrible; it falls
say as a three on a scale of zero to ten?
Shakespeare went out drinking, caught a fever,
ding! Odds are we'll be addled —
what kind of number can be put on that?
One with endless decimals,
unless you luck into some kind woman,
maker of the minimum wage, black or brown and brave enough
to face your final wreck? My friends hoard pills

for their bad news, but I wonder if it's cowardly
to be unequal to the future. Someone should write a book
for nursery school, with crucial facts like: how,
as the sun drops, shadows lengthen, including a sharp
or blurry one that is your own. And you scuttle from it
like a cockroach fleeing light — an anti-roach,
running from the dark. See my feelers, long and feathery:
I am more than well prepared.
Ulysses Grant lay in misery for half a year
after eating a peach that pained his tongue.
Versus Ivan the Terrible, last heard singing in the bath,
who fainted dead while setting up the chessboard.

Wheel

I sat, as I do, in the shallows of the lake —

after crawling through the rotting milfoil on the shore.
At first
the materials offered me were not much —

just some cattails where a hidden bullfrog croaked
and a buckhouse made from corrugated tin —

at first I thought I'd have to write the poem of its vapors.
But wait
long enough and the world caves in,

sends you something like these damselflies
prickling your chest. And the great ventriloquist
insists

you better study them or else:

how the liquidmetal blue gleams like a motorcycle helmet,
how the markings on the thorax wend like a maze,

their abdomens ringed like polecat tails,
the tip of his latched
to the back of her neck

while his scrawny forelegs wipe his mandible
that drops and shuts like a berth on a train.

But when I tallied his legs, he already had six —

those wiper-legs belonged to a gnat
he was cramming in his mouth. Which took a long time

because the gnat struggled, and I tried to imagine
a gnat-size idea of the darkness
once the mandible closed.

Call me bad gnat: see how every other thing strives —
more life!
Even with just two neurons firing the urge.

Then the she-fly's abdomen swung forward
to take the sperm packet from his thorax,
and he finished chewing

in this position that the field guide calls *The Wheel*.

Call me the empress of the unused bones,
my thighs fumigated by the rank detritus of the shore

while the meal
and The Wheel
interlocked in a chain

in the blue mouth of the sky
in the blacker mouth beyond

while I sat, as I do, in the shallows of the lake
where sixty thousand damselflies

were being made a half inch from my heart.

Pioneer

Let's not forget the Naked Woman is still out there, etched
into her aluminum plaque
affixed to her rocket
slicing through the silk of space.
In black and white, in *Time*, we blast her

off to planets made of gases and canals,
not daring to include, where her legs fork,
the little line to indicate she is an open vessel.
Which might lead to myths about her
being lined with teeth,

knives, snakes, bees — an armament
flying through the firmament. Beside the man
who stands correctly nonerect, his palm
upraised to show he comes in peace,
though you globulous yet advanced beings

have surely taken a gander of our sizzling planet
and can see us even through our garments.
So you know about the little line —
how a soft animal cleaves from her
and how we swaddle it in fluff,

yet within twenty years we send it forth
with a shoulder-mounted rocket-propelled grenade launcher:
you have probably worked out a theory
to explain the transformation. And you
have noticed how she looks a bit uncertain

as she stands on her right leg, her left thrust out
as if she's put her foot on top of something
to keep it hidden. Could be an equation
on a Post-it, or could be a booby trap—
now comes time to admit we do not know her very well, she

who has slipped the noose of our command. Be careful
when you meet her, riding on her shaft of solar wind:
you will have to break her like a wishbone
to get her open, she whom we filled with teeth
and knives and snakes and bees.

300D

When he was flush, we ate dinner
at Tung Sing on Central Avenue
where my father liked the red-dye-number-toxic
bright and shiny food: spareribs, sweet-
and-sour pork — what else
was there to care about, except his sleep
under the pup tent of the news? And the car,
which was a Cadillac until he saw how they
had become the fortresses of pimps —
our hair may look stylish now,
but in the photograph it always turns against us:
give it time and it will turn. Maybe it was in 1976
he went to see the enemy, the man
(with sideburns) who sold German cars
and said: take it easy, step at a time,
see how the diesel engine sounds
completely different. So off he went tink-tink-tink
around the block in the old neighborhood
where he imagined people (mostly black: by now
his mouth had mastered the word's exhale,
then cut) lifting their heads to look (-*kuh*).
And he, a short man, sat up taller as he swung
back into the lot to make the deal, although
to mitigate the shift in his allegiances
(or was this forgiveness? — for the Germans
had bombed his boat as he sailed through Gibraltar)
he kept the color constant. *Champagne,*
the color of a metal in a dream, no metal
you could name, although they tried

with a rich man's drink. He could afford it now
though it made him feel a little silly, his hand a lump
of meat around the glass's narrow, girlish stem.

Lubricating the Void

Heidemarie Stefanyshyn-Piper: I can barely pronounce your name
but have been thinking of you ever since your grease gun
erupted into space. Causing your tool bag to slip

beyond the reach of your white glove, when you were attempting
to repair the space station's solar wing. Thanks
for that clump of language — *solar wing!* One of the clumps

of magic shat out by our errors. And thanks
to your helmet camera's not getting smeared,
in the inch between your glove and bag — irrevocable inch —

we see the blue Earth, glowing so lit-up'dly despite the crap
that we've dumped in its oceans, a billion tons of plastic beads,
precursors to the action figures that come with our Happy Meals.

Precursors to the modern Christmas tree and handle of the modern ax.
Precursors to the belts and jackets of the vegans.
The cleanup crews call them *mermaid's tears,* as if a woman

living in the water would need to weep in polymer
so that her effort would not be lost/so that there would be proof
of her lament, say for the great Trash Vortex

swirling in the current, for the bellies of the albatrosses
filling up with tears that can't be broken down.
For the smell of mildew in the creases of ruptured beach balls,

for seabirds strangled by what makes the six-pack possible,
for flip-flops that wash up so consistently alone
they cause disturbing dreams about one-legged tribes

(described by Pliny before he sailed across the Bay of Naples,
into Mount Vesuvius's toxic spume).
Dreams logical, Heidemarie, given the fearful data.

Dreams had by us who live 220 miles below.
Queasy from our spinning but still holding on,
with no idea we are so brightly shining.

Freak-Out

Mine have occurred in empty houses
down whose dark paneling I dragged my fingernails —

though big-box stores have also played their parts,
as well as entrances to indistinct commercial buildings,

cubes of space between glass yellowing like onionskin,
making my freak-out obscure.

♦ ♦ ♦

Suddenly the head is being held between the hands
arranged in one of the conventional configurations:

hands on ears or hands on eyes
or both stacked on the forehead

as if to squeeze the wailing out,
as if the head were being juiced.

♦ ♦ ♦

The freak-out wants wide open space,
though the rules call for containment —

there are the genuine police to be considered,
which is why I recommend the empty vestibule

though there is something to be said for freaking-out
if the meadow is willing to have you

facedown in it,
mouth open to the dry summer dirt.

• • •

When my friend was freaking-out inside my car, I said
she was sitting in the freak-out's throne,

which is love's throne, too, so many fluids
from within the body on display

outside the body until the chin gleams
like the extended shy head of a snail! Even

without streetlamps, even in the purplish
penumbra of the candelabra of the firs.

• • •

My friend was freaking-out about her freak-outs,
which happened in the produce aisle;

I said: oh yeah at night, it's very
freak-inducing when the fluorescent lights

arrest you to make their interrogation! Asking
why you can't be more like the cabbages,

stacked precariously
yet so cool and self-contained,

or like the peppers who go through life
untroubled by their freaky whorls.

◆ ◆ ◆

What passes through the distillery of anguish
is the tear without the sting of salt — dripping

to fill the test tube of the body
not with monster potion but the H Two... oh, forget it...

that comes when the self is spent.
How many battles would remain

in the fetal pose if the men who rule would rip
their wool suits from their chests like girls

in olden Greece? If the bomberesses
stopped to lay their brows down on a melon.

If the torturer would only
beat the dashboard with his fists.

Maypole

Now the tanagers have returned to my dead plum tree —
they sip the pond through narrow beaks.
Orange and yellow, this recurrence
that comes with each year's baby leaves.
And if the tree is a church and spring is Sunday,
then the birds are fancy hats of women breaking into song.

Or say the tree is an old car whose tank is full,
then the birds are the girls on a joyride
crammed in its seats. Or if the tree is the carnival
lighting the tarmac of the abandoned mall by the freeway,
then the birds are the men with pocketknives
who erect its Ferris wheel.

Or say the tree is the ship that chugs into port
to fill its deck with Doug fir logs,
then the birds are the Russian sailors who
rise in the morning in the streets where they've slept,
rubbing their heads and muttering
these words that no one understands.

Les Dauphins

The dogs of the childless are barely dogs.
From tufted pillows, they rule the kingdom.
They'd stand for their portraits
in velvet suits, if they had suits —
holding hats with giant feathers.

And ousting the question: who loves the dog more?
the question becomes: whom does the dog love?
The woman says: you are the one who plays him
a drum, you tap the anthem on his head.
No, the man says, you debone him the hen,
you tie the bow of his cravat.

The dogs of the childless sleep crosswise in bed,
from human hip to human hip — a canine wire
completes the circuit. The man says: I wonder
what runs through his head
when he squeaks and snorls all through his dream?
And the woman says: out
of the dream, I'm in his dream,
riding the hunt in my lovely saddle.

When the masters are gone, the dogs of the childless
stand in the mirror with swords on their hips.
They'd stand for their portraits with dogs of their own
if we were kings, if they weren't dogs.

The Unturning

for Ben S., 1936–2010

My friend said: write about the dog in *The Odyssey*—
four hundred pages in. I found him lying on a dungheap
where ticks sipped his blood, though in his youth
he'd taken down wild animals, eager to kill
for a man the gods favored! Who comes back
in disguise; you expect the dog to give him away
with a lick or a yip, but this is not what happens.
Instead we're told that "death closed down his eyes"
the instant he saw his master after twenty years away.
And I wondered if my friend had played a trick—

setting me up with this dog who does not do much
but die. When the gods turn away, what can we do
but await their unturning? That means: don't think
that after so many years of having such a hard pillow,
the dog wasn't grateful. But I wonder
if, for the sake of the shape of the plot,
the author ought to have let him remain
for another line or two, if only to thump again his tail.

Bats

Light leaves the air like silty water
through a filterpaper sieve:
there is a draft created by its exodus
that you might think that if you rode
you too could slip away quite easily.

Is this why they call to mind the thought of death?
Squeak squeak, their song: I want to go
but I am stuck here, it is a mistake
being incarnate; I should be made
of the same substance as the dark.

If they must stay, like us they will be governed
by their hungers, pursuit
without rest. What you see in their whirling
is not purity of spirit. Only appetite,
infernal appetite — driving them, too, on.

This Red T-Shirt

was a gift from Angus, came with his new Harley
which no ladies deigned to perch their buttocks on
and was therefore sold minus the shirt—
net cost: three thousand dollars, I wear the money
in my sleep. The black braid flowing from the man

herding dice at the Squaxins' Little Creek Casino
cost me two hundred thirty-five, well worth it
for the word *croupier*. Work seven months on a poem,
then you tear it up, this does not pencil out
especially for my mother who ate potatoes

every day from 1935 to '41. Who went to the famous
Jackson Pollock show after the war — sure, she was a rube
from across the Harlem River, snickering
at the swindle of those dribbles until death squelched the supply
and drove the prices up. I've known men

who gave up houses worth half a million just to see
the back of someone whom they once bought diamonds.
And I've known women to swallow diamonds
just to amplify the spectacle of their being flushed.
The Gutenberg Bible — okay, I get that:

five-point-four million dollars for a book of poems
written by God on the skin of a calf. A hundred years ago
the Squaxins could tell you easily
who the rich man was. He'd be dressed in a red robe
made of epaulets from redwing blackbird wings.

The Wolves of Illinois

When I stopped along the road and climbed the platform that the wildlife people
built, I saw the dead grass moving. A darker gold that broke free from the pale
gold of the field.

"Wolves," said the man who stood beside me on the platform. On his other side
stood his wife and children, I assumed, dressed as if they'd come from church,

a boy and girl, her scalp crosshatched with partings from her braids. Note that this
is my way of announcing they were black

or African American, I am shy not only of the terminology but of the subject
altogether

compounded by the matter of words, *black* being strong

if not so precise a descriptor —

and my being torn about the language makes me nervous from the start. "Look at
the wolves," he told his children

before dropping a quarter in the scope, which I didn't need because I had my own
binoculars

and know the names and field marks of the birds

(like the white rump of the marsh hawk),

so I include "the white rump of the marsh hawk" as it flies over the field.

"Those are coyotes," I said

with pity for the man's foolishness? Is there a correlation between my knowledge and my pity

(an inside joke: the marsh hawk's having been renamed the *northern harrier*,

though *marsh hawk* is stronger)?

Plus what about the man's pity for the white girl with *coyote* in her mouth

—*coyote* in two syllables, the rancher's pronunciation,

when *wolf* is stronger. I wondered whether he was saving face before his family when he said, "No, those are wolves,"

or did he only want his kids to feel the dangerous elation of the word?

I could not tell because they did not look at me, they who had come from praying to a God in whom I don't believe, though I am less smug about that not-belief

(could be wrong, I oftentimes suspect)

than I am about the wolves. Because I know the wolves were coyotes;

the wolves were coyotes

and so I said, "There are no wolves in Illinois."

"No, those are wolves," the man said, turning toward his wife who offered me her twisted smile, freighted with pity or not I couldn't tell, the pity directed toward me another thing I couldn't tell, or toward her husband

the believer in wolves

(at least he was sticking by them, having staked his claim).

In the autumn withering, the eyes of the children were noticeably shin-ing, but I saw only the sidelong long-lashed white part of their eyes as they stepped up to the scope.

"Check out the wolves," he said (the minutes ticking)

(the minutes nuzzling one another's flanks)

(the minutes shining in the farthest portion of the field

as whatever emerged from the tall grass entered it again).

Pharaoh

In the saltwater aquarium at the pain clinic
lives a yellow tang
who chews the minutes in its cheeks
while we await our unguents and analgesics.

The big gods offer us this little god
before the turning of the locks
in their Formica cabinets
in the rooms of our interrogation.

We have otherwise been offered magazines
with movie stars whose shininess
diminishes as the pages lose
their crispness as they turn.

But the fish is undiminishing, its face
like the death mask of a pharaoh,
which remains while the mortal face
gets disassembled by the microbes of the tomb.

And because our pain is ancient,
we too will formalize our rituals with blood
leaking out around the needle
when the big gods try but fail

to find the bandit vein. It shrivels when pricked,
and they'll say *I've lost it*
and prick and prick until the trouble's brought
to the pale side of the other elbow

from *On the Spectrum of Possible Deaths*

from which I turn my head away—
but Pharaoh you do not turn away.
You watch us hump past with our walkers
with the tennis balls on their hind legs,

your sideways black eye on our going
down the corridor to be caressed
by the hand with the knife and the hand with the balm
when we are called out by our names.

Samara

1.
At first they're yellow butterflies
whirling outside the window —

but no: they're flying seeds.
An offering from the maple tree,

hard to believe the earth-engine capable of such invention,
that the process of mutation and dispersal
will not only formulate the right equations

but that when they finally arrive they'll be so
...*giddy?*

2.
Somewhere Darwin speculates that happiness
should be the outcome of his theory —

those who take pleasure
will produce offspring who'll take pleasure,

though he concedes the advantage of the animal who keeps death in mind
and so is vigilant.

And doesn't vigilance call for
at least an ounce of expectation,
imagining the lion's tooth inside your neck already,

for you to have your best chance of outrunning the lion

on the arrival of the lion.

3.
When it comes time to "dedicate the merit"
the Buddhists chant *from the ocean of samsara*
may I free all beings —

at first I misremembered, and thought
the word for the seed the same.

Meaning "the wheel of birth and misery and death,"
nothing in between the birth and death but misery,

surely an overzealous bit of whittlework
on the part of *Webster's Third New International Unabridged*

(though if you eliminate dogs and pie and swimming
feels about right to me —

oh shut up, Lucia. The rule is: you can't nullify the world
in the middle of your singing).

4.
In the Autonomous Vehicle Laboratory
RoboSeed is flying.
It is not a sorrow though its motor makes an annoying sound.

The doctoral students have calculated
the correct thrust-to-weight ratio and heave dynamics.
On YouTube you can watch it flying in the moonlight
outside the engineering building with the fake Ionic columns.

I said "sorrow" for the fear that in the future all the beauties
will be replaced by replicas that have more glare and blare and bling.
RoboSeed, RoboRose, RoboHeart, RoboSoul—

this way there'll be no blight
on any of the cherished encapsulations

when the blight was what we loved.

5.
They grow in chains from the bigleaf maple, chains
that lengthen until they break.
In June,

when the days are long and the sky is full
and the swept pile thickens
with the ones grown brown and brittle—

oh see how I've underestimated the persistence
of the lace in their one wing.

6.
Is there no slim chance I will feel it

when some molecule of me
(annealed by fire, like coal or glass)

is drawn up in the phloem of a maple
(please scatter my ashes under a maple)

so my speck can blip out
on a stem sprouting out of the fork of a branch,

the afterthought of a flower
that was the afterthought of a bud,

transformed now into a seed with a wing,
like the one I wore on the tip of my nose

back when I was green.

New Poems

But inside me something hopeful and insatiable —
A girl, a grown-up, giggling, gray-haired girl —
Gasps: "More, more!"

RANDALL JARRELL

Daisies vs. Bees

Who could not love the Shasta daisies, lining the walk,
the difficult daisies,
the first difficulty being that they smell like rotting meat?
Okay, you can say the smell teaches us that there is more to summer
than girls in yellow bathing suits and new-mown grass —
      if you want the beauty you have to take a whiff of death.
Okay, I know, I am not a baby:
      dear Mother Nature,
deliver me the contract and I will sign.
The second difficulty being that they attract the bees
to which a person can be fatally allergic, though
okay, it titillates, checking the mailbox in August,
a game of agility and speed,
      the goal being to outwit the feral mind.

Okay, I admit I've thought of dousing myself with perfume
      to tilt the game in their direction.
I call this "going to the bees" —
      didn't Robert Lowell say, if people were equipped with switches,
      who wouldn't be tempted, at some point,
to flick themselves off?
I admit I have romantic ideas about lying down in blossoms, though
      okay, at the first tingle of my windpipe's swelling shut, I *think*
I'd grab the EpiPen and jab the needle in my thigh.
I call this "going to the flowers" —
and in my conjuration of the jab,
I am as impassive as a samurai, outside among the daisies,
      because you have to show the bees you have no fear.
As the daisies smear everything with their odor,

how do we decide who wins, given that the bees offer us
just their speeding particles
versus the steadfast flowers?

      Given that the eyes somehow or other will close, but,
okay, okay, we know the nose will never?

Bruce

Now the world is thinner and wider: each day brings information,
such as the name of the famous mechanical shark.
Did you know sharks have two pseudopenises?
The facts come on a cable, they come from a cloud,
they come from Edith Hamilton. The biggest penis
belongs to a barnacle, at 40× its body size; it also
changes sex, à la Tiresias, when he saw two snakes
coupling and struck them with his staff.

Once I followed a small bird into the woods,
took notes on it for hours. Or I stood on a glacier,
staring into a blue crack whose dark was a long way down.
My thoughts were narrow: how not to fall in,
one inch left, one inch right, the big nada
or not. But now
                                    I move by sideways slip,
the way Tiresias skids from a prick to a slit...
then back, when he sees those snakes again —
such horny snakes! Slip far enough,
you'll go all the way around and arrive
back where you started, with two penises
also possessed by snakes, the second one
to fire off a plug so nothing else gets in!
In a similar vein, said William James:
Wisdom is learning what to overlook, but who
has the discipline to zone the *hemipenes*
outside her cranium? There's a lot of data
to be gathered until the power grid
goes down. Or the Lord comes with his airship.
Sometimes I dream I'm climbing the glacier

until I remember I can't, and turn into a worm
in a goose-down suit. Edith Hamilton
you can google. There's even reception
on top of the glacier, on top of the world —
a man can phone his mother while he freezes.
But how does a worm dial, even in a dream?

Blacktail

Like webworms, we cover the landscape with mesh
because of the deer, the ravenous deer.
They enter the yard with the footwork
of cartoon thieves — the stags wearing preposterous
inverse chandeliers, the does bearing fetuses
visibly kicking inside their cage. And who
can not-think of that crazy what-if: what if
a hoof tears through? Would you call
the dogcatcher or an ambulance?

The problem's their scale — you might as well park
a Cadillac in the house. Or go be a hunter
inside a big plastic goose, a fiberglass burger
on top of a hamburger stand. The way they tiptoe
past the bird feeder, rattling the seed
the squirrels have spilled. Then they eat
something outrageous, like the pansy
all the way up on the stoop. Before they leap
into the ravine with a noise like cymbals!

But isn't that how things end, with a cymbal crash? Leaving
you at the window with not even your rage.
Because you cannot rage at such delicate skeletons —
that is a social misdemeanor — though they have stepped
toward us the way the founding fathers
must have once approached the natives, with their arms
extended, though they bore disease.

The Great Wave

Life on this earth has often been disturbed by dreadful events

GEORGES CUVIER, 1825

1.

Now that we've entered the wave of extinction
let's sing while we still can,

before we all go where the dinosaurs went,
dropping our bones down into the shale —

and the floor of the sea becomes the top
of the mountain, the top
of the mountain the trough of the ditch.
Quick

climb onto my back and cry *wreck it wreck it*
like a frog in the grip of ecstatic amplexus

— before the UVB exceeds the threshold
or the chytrid fungus destroys our skin
or trematodes further encyst in our limb buds
or the meteor hits and Earth is once
more wrapped in a cloak of dust.

2.

Please accept my regret
for the frogs that I've eaten
but grant me the gig
with which I impaled them

and the words *gig* and *impale*
and especially the splashing through
the lake edge at night
searching for eyes!

There was too much to love about their deaths,
using the gig like a picador

stabbing the hump on the neck of the bull
so the darkness roars and throws down its roses!

At least, I felt its velvet petals on my cheeks.

   3.
This year's Christmas trees are tainted
with Pacific chorus frogs

that we're not supposed to let hop
out the door. But there's an easy solution:

all you need is a jar.
And the will
to stick the jar in the freezer

overnight
then flush.
It's simple, it's clean.

No one's talking about a whale here
dead in the dooryard.

Or an aurochs or a quagga.

4.

Too late for the golden toads, who vanished
as soon as the scientists arrived to map out
their plots. Until it dawned
on the scientists: *they*
were the vector. As in:

Look for me under your bootsoles.
You will hardly know who I am or what I mean,
But I shall filter and fiber your blood.

But in the village you can still buy
figurines, for luck — golden toads
on cell phones and toads on mopeds and toads

who will serenade you with their mandolins.

5.

I don't have the ending: ask the Vegas Valley leopard frog.
The dwarf hippopotamus or the giant swan.
Stag-moose, shrub-ox, passenger pigeon.
The golden coquí or the short-faced bear.

When we are gone, may some survivor
like Mr. Industrious Roach
evolve enough to hawk our likenesses
for didn't we cherish commerce and
view fortune as a wheel.

Water Theory

Now I live where I see water — you pay more
to see water. Perhaps the eye prefers the subtlety
of liquid to the commotion of the leaves,
which right now are yellow and spotted,
about to spring into the air. Whereas the water
features nothing falling nothing dying,
its surface made dark or light by clouds
as they sweep past — though they too
decompose when raked by wind, or when the sun
rides in like a warlord in his jeep.

Or could be that we prefer the water
for its resemblance to money, a thin array of coins.
The gray is common; it's the glimmer that's rare,
as the red semicircle on the blackbird's wing
was once prized by native people of the West
in the absence of the cardinal.

Two theories. Now I am out of theories.

Save for one claiming the flat expanse
is also a stage where the self steps out.
And we think the feeling of the body
as hollow as a nutshell or a husk
is the product of threatening it with many
cubic yards of sky, not that it's finally secured somewhere
to rehearse its final bow.

Elegy for Idle Curiosity

I used to ask aloud such things as: *why is the moon round,*
buffed only by the chamois cloth of space?
But now I hold my tongue, or else people start to tap
apparatuses they've strapped to their hips
as if they were knights. They *are* knights,
assailed by the uncertain. When it stands to reason
that we must be somewhere on the map: the self
tends to be the only one not knowing where it is.

No more paddling the murk of pointless speculation,
wondering whether the force that stirs the whirlpool
also winds the spider's web. A person can't just wobble around
with her mouth open — it arouses
the surveillance. Instead we're supposed to be
like traffic lights, vigilant in every season.
No more standing like a chanterelle, spewing out ten thousand spores,
penetrating the substrate, laying a fiber everywhere.

Belated Poem in the Voice of the Pond

Time to snuff the candles of the lily pads.

The newts that all summer long
plied thick water with their toe-tips splayed
have dug their own graves

in the dust-brown bottom.
Painted turtles hold their positions
on a log: they are moon rocks

detained by the sun.

The naked trees look muscular
and when bent by the wind
they push back

though their limbs drop off
little by lot. And this time of year
inside each branch you can see

the red fuse, smoldering.

for Hayden Carruth, in memoriam

Early December, Two Weeks Shy

There's a rectangle of oily substrate where the garden grew,
a greasy vine impounded by each tomato cage
someone meant to store in the shed but somehow the months
just slipped…

no point to hauling them in now
since the days will soon be lengthening again, *oh slide me in*
to this dark trench on the backward side of autumn
and then just let me sleep…

Only the brussels sprouts are lit on their bright leathery tree
unravaged by the slugs,
unmildewed by the rain.
Siphoning the sheen

off the day's gray skin,
not suffering from the season
though they dwell among the spores.
Go on, ask how this is possible, however childish it may be

to address the little green bulbs
of their undistinguished brains.
The days will only dim before they brighten;
other friends have taken to their beds.

*Speckled and Silver

I have read a lot of books and most of them I have forgotten,
in particular one about a man who grew up on a farm
or was it ranch in Reno or maybe it was Oregon —
one thing that's clear is that I read it
lying on the sofa in the Quince Street house
while a particular light* washed over me
that made me realize snow had begun to fall.
Sometime around December '97,
though in the book it was I think spring in '53:
as I turned pages I heard the rusty gears
inside the world also struggling to turn.
Time folded then like a musty old quilt
someone had laid me to bed underneath:
I was reading, or was I dreaming I was reading,
other duties suspended, badges removed,
hat on a hook, resignation turned in. All I had to do
was turn on a light when the blue air thickened.
That was it: to turn on a light. Either turn
on the light or just lie there in the dark.

My Only Objection

I hope the weather is good this day
we celebrate the marriage of Tom and John
now that it's legal in this state, though I worry
I'm pledging to a sorority whose mission
is making crowns from shiny things
found on the beach or bought on eBay
so all the people who are coupled
can be crowned, but that's it. Union is king
and union is queen. And one might feel
the urge to combat this insistence
by becoming a drifter. Or by joining everything
to neutralize the hierarchies
between the clouds and the jet stream,
the worm and the dirt,
one shiny fly and the other
shiny, shiny fly! Let the green blades
become one with their holes in the ground, the rootlets
their nutrients, the ant its labor,
the fir needle it carries, the ant the path
it trudges along. Couple the chlorophyll
and the leaf to the light, the skull
to the sky, the frog to the lily,
lily to pond, fly to the frog, yes and even
the frog to the snake. Let us wed
our intestines to cake, the dog
to the bone, spider to web,
man to man and human to human and
creature to creature, and creature
to dust, and all the particles

to all of the waves and quark to quark
and vibrating string to vibrating string
to vibrating string till everything
hums with being crowned.

FREE

Found this old photo album by the road
in a box that also contained an eggbeater
and a pair of skates. Its white vinyl cover
stamped in gold *OUR WEDDING* —

first page heavy parchment, rain-rumpled
but stiff, with spaces for names,
dates, all the facts
you would not want to forget—all these

left blank. But before we rush
to unhappy conclusions, let me say
it is not such an uncommon thing
to not do, filling in blanks

required in so many ominous settings
that to require it of love
may not seem the work of happy gods.
Who is to say the final vinyl sleeves

foretell any type of troubled uncoupling
just because they are empty?
The inevitable dispersals —
the wayfarer also ends up by the road —

and look: he's whistling. It is natural
that black turns brown and white goes yellow
as the atmosphere spins
against the gold letters. Every object selected

and carried away as the hawkweed
turns into a ball of achenes
at the base of the Stop sign, where the box
is dissolved by the next season.

Eschatological

When the old man said the woodpecker was gone for good,
I told him no, the experts found one
down in the bayou, where had he been?

So big that when men saw it overhead
they were said to call out for the Lord.

We must not think the worst of the world, I said
because the old man could be a grumbler, one of those
who say that mankind feeds on what is beautiful
and excretes shopping malls

(well he has never had to buy a curler).

But now the experts have retracted their discovery
and it's the old man who's gone for good
and the one thing that endures it seems:

those sixty-something ivory-billed woodpeckers
dead in shallow drawers at Harvard
in the Museum of Natural History. Study specimens
for which you do not need a natural pose, it's more
this thing is dead, let's not pretend we didn't kill it.

Bird after bird — and your heart ambushed
by their conformity when one by one
those drawers come rolling out.

Suddenly they're smaller than they were.

And how do you explain the parallax?
No, you cannot, so roll the drawer back in.

A Little Death, Suitable for Framing

T (the Nobel laureate)
warns us to be on the lookout
for a tailor,
not the Reaper.

We will know him by his well-made
but shabby suit.

And the sharp implement he carries
turns out to be a needle.
In the gloaming we might see its tip,
a speck of light
created by the moon.

Its long thread, of course,
will not be visible.

Until he gets up close.

Etiology of my illness (I ran the nature center near the city, so

the cause could be the boy or the river or the snakes —
all of them left a musky grease on my skin.
The garter snakes' teeth left tiny red pinpricks;
I liked to show off my not-flinching when they bit me on the arm.

All of them left a greasy musk on my skin,
starting with the boys, with their pleas and their diseases.
I liked to show off my not-flinching when they bit me on the arm
in those days when we thought penicillin or abortion could fix all scenarios

starting with the boys, with their pleas and their diseases.
No one worried much about the porous membranes
in those days when we thought penicillin or abortion could fix all scenarios —
fat chance. I tried to prove myself by swimming far into the river.

No one worried much about the porous membranes
even as the body-boat let down its gangplank for the germs.
Fat chance I proved myself by swimming far into the river
whose water's clean now, though its bed was found to be a little toxic still.

Even as the body-boat let down its gangplank for the germs
the garter snakes' teeth left tiny red pinpricks.
Now my bed is clean, but the snakes were found to be a little toxic. Still:
the cause could be the river or the boy who dropped me on my head.)

Rotator Cuff Vortex

for Tim Kelly

When the TV played above the bar, I faked my interest in the game —
it was the bodies that I wanted to tell the stories. Like the story
Tim told of Darryl Stingley: there was a photo of him playing
in his obituary, leaping for the football
in a perfect arabesque (this before the hit that cut
his spinal cord). On Friday nights, Tim and his friends throw

the Vortex ball in the bookstore parking lot, although Tim threw
his shoulder out, and now the game
is on hold until the surgeon finds the time to cut
Tim's rotator cuff and reattach the fittings. The body tells a story
mostly about loss (all, in Stingley's case). And still the ball
exerts a pull: the men strain toward it when the TV's playing,

transfixing the dog as well, who goes crazy playing
fetch, and will retrieve as long as anyone can be coerced to throw,
a drive inbred and neural, although the ball
is, in the dog's case, a stand-in for some specimen of game —
by what gene does the compulsion travel? In the epic story
of the Maya, the heroes get their necks cut

by the wings of bats down in the underworld, so that their cut
heads can bounce off the hips of the death-lords playing
what is simply called "the ball game" — naturally, the story
ends with the heroes resurrected, then thrown
into the sky to become the moon and sun. Scholars call the game
a way of ritualizing war, blood not entirely averted by the ball

since the losers were beheaded, skulls racked like bowling balls
in the upperworld arena. I have seen depictions of this cut
into the stones of Chichén Itzá, where you can hear the game
still roaring from the dusty court, although the playing
died five hundred years ago. Also carved there is the throne,
or chacmool, and the king lounging on it, though this story

is debated: could be any doofus spectating. And what's the story
behind his enthrallment with the ball —
do all round things have gravity, no matter if they're thrown
by men or spin of their own accord in space, orbs cut
from bigger orbs in a motion picture that's been playing
ever since The Bang? And we take our minuscule positions in the game.

Forever after, Stingley sat in the throne of his chair, uncomplaining,
probably dumbstruck: your old life cuts out and a story takes over
that's all a game played by the ball on your neck.

Message Unscripted

November flung from summer's flywheel,
the plants on the porch gone leggy and brown, and moldy
from the damp. *Don't stick your head in a plastic bag*
the spiders say, you think I'm being whimsical but I say
they say it in these webs besilvered with rain, two
hanging side by side from the railing, another two
strung perpendicular, one from the dying potted peony,
one from the dying potted dahlia. ART SAVES LIVES
says the bumper on my neighbor's truck, and though
I always thought that was just an example of liberal
arts professors' taking liberties, it could refer to this
minor rehabilitation of the season. So for its service,
let's dedicate the next fifty-two seconds to art,
how all things make it, both arachnid ribosomes and rain.
Think of a cloud, think of a geode, think of the mold
on the plate in the fridge. This strange assemblage
made by weather and an arthropod: what fates conspired,
whose mind was at work, or did it result from a force
from before the first bang? Spiders themselves
don't appear to ask, and don't think
that's because they lack the intellectual chops — just imagine
what concentration of mind it would take
to wait unmoving in your own fiber installation,
hours spent with your legs so artfully outsplayed?

Women in Black

I'm talking about the ones who trawled the thoroughfare
in dark garments whose long hems
were coming loose — had you seen them
or did you dream them? For sure
you whispered their mythology in the dirt rut
underneath the monkey bars: the husbands
who had lain down on the tracks, or the kids
with too much skull above their brows —
being jilted at the courthouse,
blackmailed by ghosts, afflictions caused
by criminals who found them when the men
were working late. Hair snarled and wild
or pinned up too severely, necks bent
so they could scrutinize the minutiae
(a metal thimble or a garter clip)
washed up by the curb. Things lasted
longer, rotted quicker, the materials
were better, the technology was worse.
But were they real, or only forms
to fear becoming, gossip of the yellow bus,
feral wisdom, mother-lore, stepdaughters of Carl Jung?
Who made them wander, was it you,
from Yonkers to Sleepy Hollow, gathering
bouquets of weeds and resting on public benches
whose slats cried out for paint? Their legs
splintered, grief-thinned, lorn — their hands
(preternaturally large) you feared: that one
might clap itself to you in passing,
that she might begin to speak.

The Rape of Blanche DuBois

What did I know about art? I had seen a few foreign movies, that was it.

When I drove from my childhood home, I reached the Cuyahoga River and was disappointed to find it not burning because I knew a song about its burning. When I came to the Platte River I was satisfied because the song I knew was about a bum along its bank, and I did see that.

I thought a river burning would be art. A bum along a river could be art, with the right sort of lighting, but the man I saw was not correctly lit.

Nearby however was a warehouse, where a local troupe was putting on *A Streetcar Named Desire*. The word *streetcar* made me think of hats, and stockings that hooked onto garter belts.

Plus, *desire* was a word with its own little jet-plane that could whisk you off to Paris.

So I parked by a drainpipe running down the wall where the poster had been pasted. It showed a woman being eaten by a shadow.

Not a gray one but a black.

Inside, the warehouse was cold despite the rumble of the heater, and as soon as she stepped onto the stage, you knew that Blanche was damaged. I remember wanting to tell her that we didn't have to do this, enact her humiliation. And my simultaneous wanting her to do exactly that.

Break into little pieces, like the bits that are fed to dogs. *Ah!* I thought, *so this is Art*. This chewing, my cheeks full of Blanche.

And when he was finally alone with her, in this production Stanley tore off his silk pajamas. Turned away from me, but still: I remember all the muscles in the actor's rump.

A muscled rump aroused me even as it horrified.

Then the warehouse went black for the scene change, a few moments of dark during which my arousal deflated. You may not believe me when I say the air expelled by its deflation was sufficient to eject me — from one life into another, into my authentic life, in those black moments that contained both the ardor and the horror, and the wonder at their having been simultaneously created.

When the lights came up again, the men in the white coats hauled her off, The End. And as we clapped, everyone sheepishly stole a glance or two, to check the status of everyone else's arousal. Asking *which life are you in? your old life or your new?*

The new one that was the product of your willingness to be manipulated, and therefore of your gullibility,

or the old one that is childish, or at least naive.

Either answer was defective, which is why we looked down at our feet as we moved toward the exits. Outside I was glad to have only the stars' lighting me with their white needles.

What I Know

The enemy is a place over there
somewhere, it's easy to get confused
now that the countries have been renamed
and their boundaries redrawn—
in fact it may be over, I am not sure,
the war's been (or had been) waging
so long that I'd forgotten about it;
I am embarrassed to admit my memory
is no longer what it once was. I don't
want to make excuses for myself, but
there also used to be a lot more hubbub
on the streets that would remind you,
people either kissing choreographically
or chanting singsongs learned in high school
at the pep rallies, the words slightly
altered. Who understands
what they are saying? — Sorry, but I do not hear
so well since while it rages
(raged) I seem to have become
an old woman whose television still
has an antenna whose only news is snow.

Time Will Clean the Carcass Bones

1.

It starts with a dead animal: whenever she finds one
when walking the dogs up in the hills,
Jane puts the carcass in a cage on the roof
in order to bring up the bone-curls and -fractals.

Otherwise she'd have to dig
slantwise through the manglement; it's best
to leave that to the professionals, the sun
and the maggots, the distant star and the grub inside,
best to put on some music. Best not to listen
for any decibels of little mandibles.

2.

Such an old old problem, what to do with the meat,
you would think by now we could just go poof.
At the industrial park, the crematorium's metal walls
are lined with Sheetrock to give the illusion
they will last. Sofa in the viewing room, curtains
on the window on whose other side the human corpse
rides through unfinished space, a slow conveyor
to the oven's mouth. Stay as long as you want but be
forewarned: grief will interrupt when the curtain's closed
while someone checks the progress of the flames.

3.

Sometimes the Oglala left their dead in trees
to make it easier either (a) for the soul to revert to birdstate
or (b) for the wolves to be defeated. Women's work:
painting the body with vermilion, wrapping it

in a buffalo skin, flesh-side out. Lastly
a bright red blanket *renders the scene more picturesque*
while the women lament *wild and weird.*

If he be a brave, nest with him a few buffalo heads
which time has rendered inoffensive; if he be a chief

slay his favorite pony and lay it underneath

4.
The body's scaffold possesses such a stringent whiteness
you can easily feel aggrieved at how it's defiled
by the slackening form.

Well, the bones may have the beauty but the meat
the better story. As in: see how someone
cut off my left breast!

Versus their sterile silence. When Hamlet asks the bones
whether he should kill himself, they refuse to render an opinion,

a song that's lured even children to sing
for five hundred years without minding what it means.

5.
You cannot know when they are finished — no, you just call
it quits

depending on the whiteness you hope to arrive at,

how much stain you'll put up with

or whether you value these relics simply
for the majestic architecture of mammalian innerstructure

uncannily inputted by evolution's overmaster,

how often you know you'll look from your work to the still
some-percentage-flesh adhering to the bone, your eyes

shifting between it and the clock measuring its desiccation.

6.
But first you have to find an old toothbrush
—or failing, demote one still in use—
to scrub off the gristle that clings to the cracks
and rubbery clods that hang by a thread
before boiling them down to a stink: half-cloying,
half-sweet, every drape in the house
forever infected, even far from the bones,
with the scent of the putrid distilled from the earth,
making your fibers all mortally fragrant
with the power and glory, forever, amen.

7.
Back on the roof, the creatures march
in a synchronized procession — first blowflies and flesh flies,
then carrion beetles. The flies are so shiny

yet their young make you shiver,
waggling out of the meat as it's eaten
by these grubs who are eaten by carrion beetles.

Then the Hymenoptera wasps lay their eggs in the beetles
and also in the larvae of some of the flies,
where they grow inside the meat of the grubs
who are themselves the meat of the carrion beetles.

8.

And why the bones, not the heart, since so much is made
of that bloody mitten? It would have to float in a jar

full of poisonous murk that it casts its webs through.
And this is not the body of old anatomy books

whose drawings and colors, dotted lines, little numbers
corresponding to a column of names, all suggest

great logic and beauty, part of which surely must remain
even after the last calamity. But all this

would molder in the wide open air, where only the bones can sing.
And of course the teeth, the bones' little knives, unsheathed.

9.

Every heart sings a song that's incomplete
said Plato, until another heart whispers back.
He forgot PS: the song might not be sweet.

Plus, hearts might be what this song likes to eat:
chomp chomp. Yum yum. Its teeth could be black
with rot and you might not want to hear their incomplete

singing even if it's a song — you might not be so desperate,
maybe you find enough fulfillment in the back
catalogue of your own songs, however incomplete.
Or maybe you find completed songs too goddamned sweet.

10.

The bones will stand next to books by philosophers
and books by poets. Because you might need relief
from all that thinking, might need a pelvis for its holes

to see the sky through. You are not so different
from a coyote or a cougar; maybe you'd have been one

if your mother wore another name. And what but meat
would a cougar read? — better empty the shelves,

fill them with bones. Because the books hold in
what the bones spell out: it won't be long
before your beauty will have all the time in the world.

Yellow Claw

For weeks a backhoe has been working
where the shore drops into the bay: it claws
then lifts a yellow clawful
of rubble. Other times
the claw's being used as a sledge.

Inside the cab, we already know, there's a man,
his orange shirt visible
a long way off. The cab swings in circles
but the man never dizzies. We know this
because we never see the claw spazzing out.

How strange a translation is the world
of the mind behind the world!
The sky already darkening,
the man's belly growls, his big fat belly,
and the future he spreads with the claw's rusty teeth,

every hillock and divot, is really mashed potatoes
and gravy, the day's fixation, as he shapes the land,
tamps it in. Someday a bone will be broken here
in the bad dip, layer within the layer
someday to be sifted

and sifted again, though they slip through the mesh.
Photons, neutrinos, the governing waves —
mashed potatoes and gravy:
ever since the doctor forbade it
how he craves the salt.

Day-Moon

Driving the car, walking the dog…
cresting the hill. When suddenly
you catch sight of the day-moon: why
does it come with almost a jolt of pain?

You mean the pain inflicted by its beauty?
No, I mean the pain
caused by its having been up for hours,
and though you'd noticed, you had not seen.

Blaring at you from a sky
the blue of a fast car of a bygone day —
you have so far to go in your perceptual awakening
and the day-moon is the meter of your failings.

And if you'd seen, would you still feel
that soft and slightly sick spot in your stomach
whenever you stoop to self-reflection: now
you wouldn't stoop, being perceptually awakened

though not boastful, no never boastful.

Meanwhile the day-moon circles the globe like Superman,
hauling the seas on his white shoulders
flying half a mile a second,
taking care of business

but also as calm as the Virgin Mary.
See her face up there?
People used to say that it was made of cheese.
Such silent cheese. Such busy cheese.

About the Author

Lucia Perillo's sixth book of poems, *On the Spectrum of Possible Deaths* (Copper Canyon, 2012), was a finalist for the National Book Critics Circle Award and received the Pacific Northwest Booksellers Association Award. Her other publications include a book of stories, *Happiness Is a Chemical in the Brain* (Norton, 2012), and one of essays, *I've Heard the Vultures Singing* (Trinity University Press, 2009). *Inseminating the Elephant* (Copper Canyon, 2009) was a finalist for the Pulitzer Prize.

Copper Canyon Press is deeply grateful to

CHRIS HIGASHI

for her many years of service to poetry
and independent nonprofit publishing.

Poetry is vital to language and living. Since 1972, Copper Canyon Press has published extraordinary poetry from around the world to engage the imaginations and intellects of readers, writers, booksellers, librarians, teachers, students, and donors.

WE ARE GRATEFUL FOR THE MAJOR SUPPORT PROVIDED BY:

THE PAUL G. ALLEN
FAMILY FOUNDATION

Anonymous

Jill Baker and Jeffrey Bishop

Donna and Matt Bellew

John Branch

Diana Broze

Sarah and Tim Cavanaugh

Janet and Les Cox

Catherine Eaton and David Skinner

Mimi Gardner Gates

Linda Gerrard and Walter Parsons

Gull Industries, Inc.
on behalf of William and Ruth True

The Trust of Warren A. Gummow

Elizabeth Hebert

Steven Myron Holl

Lakeside Industries, Inc.
on behalf of Jeanne Marie Lee

TO LEARN MORE ABOUT UNDERWRITING
COPPER CANYON PRESS TITLES,
PLEASE CALL 360-385-4925 EXT. 103

WE ARE GRATEFUL FOR THE MAJOR SUPPORT PROVIDED BY:

Maureen Lee and Mark Busto

Rhoady Lee and Alan Gartenhaus

Ellie Mathews and Carl Youngmann as The North Press

Anne O'Donnell and John Phillips

Suzie Rapp and Mark Hamilton

Joseph C. Roberts

Jill and Bill Ruckelshaus

Cynthia Lovelace Sears and Frank Buxton

Kim and Jeff Seely

Dan Waggoner

Austin Walters

Barbara and Charles Wright

The dedicated interns and faithful volunteers
of Copper Canyon Press

The Chinese character for poetry is made up of two parts: "word"
and "temple." It also serves as pressmark for Copper Canyon Press.

This book is set in Whitman, developed from Kent Lew's studies
of W.A. Dwiggins's Caledonia. The heads are set in Whitney,
designed by Tobias Frere-Jones. Book design by VJBScribe.
Printed on archival-quality paper.